Shell Scripting 101

A Beginner's Guide to Bash

Kaizen Brooks

Welcome to "Shell Scripting 101: A Beginner's Guide to Bash"! In today's fast-paced digital world, automation has become a crucial skill for every aspiring programmer, system administrator, or tech enthusiast. At the heart of automation lies the powerful Bash scripting language, a tool that empowers you to harness the full potential of your computer and automate tasks with precision and efficiency.

This book is designed to be your gateway into the world of shell scripting, regardless of your prior programming experience. Whether you are a beginner eager to dip your toes into the vast ocean of scripting or an experienced programmer seeking to expand your repertoire, this guide will provide you with a solid foundation in Bash scripting.

With each turn of the page, you will embark on a journey that takes you from the fundamental concepts of shell scripting to the mastery of complex automation tasks. Through clear explanations, practical examples, and hands-on exercises, you will gradually unlock the secrets of Bash and discover its immense power.

We will begin by introducing you to the fascinating world of shell scripting, explaining its significance and exploring the versatility of the Bash shell. You will learn how to set up your shell environment, configure it to suit your needs, and navigate the command-line interface with ease.

From there, we will dive into the core principles of Bash scripting, unraveling the syntax, commands, and control structures that form the building blocks of your scripts. You will master the art of manipulating variables, making decisions with conditional statements, and automating repetitive tasks with loops.

As your knowledge and skills evolve, we will guide you through more advanced topics, such as input/output operations, text processing, file and directory manipulation, and error handling. You will explore the intricacies of function creation, understand how to work with command-line arguments, and leverage the power of regular expressions.

But this book is not just about theory and syntax. It goes beyond that. You will also discover best practices for writing clean, maintainable, and efficient code. We will equip you with debugging techniques and introduce you to a range of tools and utilities that will enhance your scripting capabilities.

Moreover, you will witness the true potential of Bash scripting as we explore its integration with the operating system, its role in process management and job control, and its ability to automate tasks on a scheduled basis.

Finally, we will address the vital aspect of script portability, guiding you on how to write scripts that can run seamlessly across different platforms and environments, ensuring your code remains flexible and adaptable.

Throughout this journey, we encourage you to engage actively, experiment with the concepts presented, and challenge yourself with the exercises provided. Remember, learning shell scripting is a hands-on endeavor, and the more you practice, the more proficient you will become.

By the end of this book, you will have gained a solid understanding of Bash scripting and the confidence to tackle real-world automation challenges. Whether you want to streamline your personal workflow, optimize system administration tasks, or impress your colleagues with your scripting prowess, this guide will equip you with the skills you need.

So, let's embark on this exciting adventure together. Welcome to the world of "Shell Scripting 101: A Beginner's Guide to Bash"! Let's unlock the potential of automation and empower ourselves to accomplish more with less effort.

Chapter 1: Introduction to Shell Scripting................... 9
    1.1 What is Shell Scripting?... 9
    1.2 Benefits and Use Cases of Shell Scripting........... 12
    1.3 Understanding the Bash Shell............................... 15
    1.4 Overview of the Bash Scripting Language............ 19

Chapter 2: Getting Started with Bash........................ 23
    2.1 Installing Bash... 23
    2.2 Launching the Bash Shell....................................... 26
    2.3 Navigating the Shell Environment.........................29
    2.4 Basic Shell Commands...32

Chapter 3: Setting Up Your Shell Environment........... 36
    3.1 Configuring Shell Preferences............................... 36
    3.2 Customizing the Shell Prompt............................... 40
    3.3 Working with Shell Configuration Files................ 43
    3.4 Managing Environment Variables......................... 46

Chapter 4: Basic Bash Commands and Syntax........... 50
    4.1 Executing Commands in the Shell........................ 50
    4.2 Command-Line Options and Arguments.............. 54
    4.3 Redirecting Input and Output................................ 57
    4.4 Pipelines and Filters... 60
    4.5 Command Substitution... 64

Chapter 5: Variables and Data Types in Bash............. 67
    5.1 Understanding Variables in Bash......................... 68
    5.2 Declaring and Assigning Variables....................... 71
    5.3 Variable Scope and Lifetime.................................. 75
    5.4 Working with Data Types: Strings, Numbers, and Arrays..78

Chapter 6: Conditional Statements and Loops........... 82
    6.1 Introduction to Conditional Statements................ 83
    6.2 The if-else Statement... 87
    6.3 The case Statement.. 89

6.4 Introduction to Looping.. 92
6.5 The for Loop... 95
6.6 The while and until Loops....................................... 98
Chapter 7: Input and Output in Shell Scripts............ 102
7.1 Reading User Input.. 103
7.2 Displaying Output to the User............................. 105
7.3 Working with Files and Directories.......................108
Chapter 8: String Manipulation and Text Processing 112
8.1 String Concatenation and Manipulation.............. 113
8.2 Pattern Matching and Substring Extraction......... 116
8.3 Text Manipulation with Regular Expressions...... 120
8.4 Using awk and sed for Text Processing.............. 123
Chapter 9: File and Directory Operations...................127
9.1 Working with Files: Creating, Reading, and Writing.. 128
9.2 File Permissions and Ownership......................... 131
9.3 File and Directory Navigation...............................134
9.4 File and Directory Manipulation........................... 137
Chapter 10: Functions and Modular Programming... 141
10.1 Introduction to Functions................................... 142
10.2 Creating and Invoking Functions....................... 145
10.3 Function Parameters and Return Values.......... 149
10.4 Organizing Code into Modules.......................... 153
Chapter 11: Error Handling and Debugging...............157
11.1 Handling Errors and Exceptions........................158
11.2 Using Exit Codes and Error Messages............. 162
11.3 Debugging Techniques and Tools..................... 166
Chapter 12: Advanced Shell Scripting Techniques...171
12.1 Advanced Control Structures: select and until.. 172
12.2 Advanced String Manipulation and Regular Expressions.. 175
12.3 Advanced File and Directory Operations.......... 178

12.4 Advanced Scripting Tools and Utilities............. 181
Chapter 13: Working with Command-Line Arguments... 185
    13.1 Introduction to Command-Line Arguments....... 186
    13.2 Parsing and Validating Command-Line Arguments 190
    13.3 Advanced Command-Line Argument Handling 194
Chapter 14: Working with Regular Expressions........199
    14.1 Introduction to Regular Expressions................200
    14.2 Pattern Matching and Regular Expression Operators... 204
    14.3 Using Regular Expressions in Bash Scripts..... 208
Chapter 15: Process Management and Job Control. 212
    15.1 Managing Processes in Bash........................... 213
    15.2 Background and Foreground Processes.......... 217
    15.3 Job Control and Process Monitoring.................221
Chapter 16: Shell Scripting Best Practices................ 225
    16.1 Writing Clear and Readable Code.................... 226
    16.2 Handling Errors and Exceptions Properly......... 231
    16.3 Code Organization and Modularization............ 236
    16.4 Optimizing Shell Script Performance................ 240
Chapter 17: Automating Tasks with Shell Scripts..... 245
    17.1 Understanding Automation and Scripting......... 246
    17.2 Creating Simple Automation Scripts................. 250
    17.3 Scheduling Scripts with cron.............................253
    17.4 Using Shell Scripts in Workflow Automation..... 257
Chapter 18: Introduction to Shell Scripting Tools and Utilities...261
    18.1 Introduction to External Commands and Utilities.... 262
    18.2 Using Standard Unix Utilities in Scripts............ 266
    18.3 Commonly Used Shell Scripting Tools and Libraries... 269

Chapter 19: Interacting with the Operating System.. 274
    19.1 Gathering System Information.......................... 275
    19.2 Managing Users and Groups............................ 279
    19.3 Interacting with Services and Daemons........... 282
    19.4 File System Operations and Permissions......... 285

Chapter 20: Writing Portable Shell Scripts................. 288
    20.1 Understanding Shell Script Portability.............. 290
    20.2 Writing POSIX-Compliant Shell Scripts............ 292
    20.3 Dealing with Platform-Specific Differences....... 296

Chapter 1: Introduction to Shell Scripting

In this chapter, we lay the foundation for your journey into the world of shell scripting. We will start by unraveling the concept of shell scripting, understanding its significance in automation, and exploring the versatility of the Bash shell. Whether you're a curious beginner or an experienced programmer looking to expand your skills, this chapter will provide you with a solid introduction to the exciting realm of shell scripting. Get ready to dive into the heart of automation and unleash the power of scripting with Bash.

1.1 What is Shell Scripting?

Shell scripting is a powerful and versatile technique used to automate tasks and create complex sequences of commands in a shell environment. A shell script is essentially a series of commands written in a scripting language that is interpreted by a shell, such as Bash (Bourne Again SHell) or other compatible shells like sh, csh, or ksh.

At its core, a shell script acts as a bridge between the user and the operating system, allowing the user to execute commands and perform operations without the need for manual intervention. It combines the functionality of a shell, which is a command-line interpreter, with the flexibility and programmability of a scripting language.

Shell scripting offers numerous advantages and use cases. It enables the automation of repetitive tasks, simplifies complex operations, and provides a way to customize and extend the capabilities of the shell environment. Shell scripts can be used for a wide range of purposes, including system administration, file and data processing, software deployment, task scheduling, and more.

One of the key benefits of shell scripting is its accessibility. Shell scripts are relatively easy to write, especially for users familiar with command-line interfaces and basic programming concepts. The scripting language used in shell scripts allows for variables, control structures (such as loops and conditional statements), functions, and file manipulation, providing a rich set of tools for scripting tasks.

Shell scripting also leverages the power of the command-line interface. By combining multiple commands and utilities within a script, users can create complex workflows and execute them with a single command. This not only saves time and effort but also ensures consistency and repeatability in executing tasks.

Moreover, shell scripting is highly portable across different systems and platforms. Shell scripts written in POSIX-compliant syntax can be executed on various operating systems, including Linux, Unix, macOS, and even Windows using shell emulators or subsystems. This portability makes shell scripts a versatile tool that can be shared and utilized across different environments.

The flexibility of shell scripting allows for the integration of external programs and utilities. Shell scripts can invoke system commands, utilize text processing tools like awk or sed, interact with databases, make network requests, and execute other scripts or programs. This integration capability enables shell scripts to extend their functionality beyond the capabilities of the shell itself.

In addition, shell scripting promotes code reusability and modularity. By organizing scripts into functions or modules, specific tasks can be encapsulated and reused across multiple scripts, promoting code maintainability and reducing redundancy.

However, it is important to note that while shell scripting is a powerful tool, it does have some limitations. Shell scripts may not be as efficient as compiled programs, especially for computationally intensive tasks. They also have limited support for complex data structures and advanced programming concepts. In such cases, higher-level languages like Python or Perl might be more suitable.

In conclusion, shell scripting is a valuable skill for automating tasks, enhancing productivity, and managing system operations. It provides a flexible and accessible way to interact with the operating system, execute commands, and create custom workflows. By harnessing the power of shell scripting, users can streamline their workflows, increase efficiency, and unlock the full potential of the command-line interface.

1.2 Benefits and Use Cases of Shell Scripting

Shell scripting offers a multitude of benefits and is widely utilized across various domains due to its versatility and practicality. Let's explore some of the key advantages and common use cases of shell scripting:

1. **Automation of Tasks**: Shell scripting excels in automating repetitive or time-consuming tasks. By writing a script to perform these tasks, you can save considerable time and effort. Whether it's generating reports, performing backups, or deploying software, shell scripts streamline operations and minimize manual intervention.

2. **Simplification of Complex Operations**: Shell scripts allow you to combine multiple commands and utilities into a single script, simplifying complex operations. This makes it easier to perform intricate tasks that involve a series of steps or require coordination between different components.

3. **System Administration**: Shell scripting is extensively used for system administration tasks. It enables administrators to manage user accounts, configure network settings, monitor system resources, install software packages, and perform system maintenance activities. Shell scripts provide a way to automate these administrative tasks and ensure consistency across multiple systems.

4. **File and Data Processing**: Shell scripts are highly effective for file and data processing tasks. They can manipulate file contents, extract specific information, search and replace text, sort and filter data, and perform various operations on files and directories. Shell scripting is particularly useful when dealing with log files, CSV or JSON data, or any text-based data processing.

5. **Task Scheduling and Cron Jobs**: Shell scripting integrates seamlessly with task scheduling mechanisms like cron jobs. With shell scripts, you can schedule recurring tasks at specific times or intervals. This is beneficial for tasks such as backups, data

synchronization, log analysis, and report generation. Shell scripts enable automated execution of these tasks without manual intervention.

6. **Customization of Shell Environment**: Shell scripting allows users to customize their shell environment. By writing scripts, you can define aliases, customize prompts, set environment variables, and create shortcuts for frequently used commands. This customization enhances productivity and personalizes the shell experience.

7. **System Monitoring and Reporting**: Shell scripts are instrumental in system monitoring and generating reports. They can collect system metrics such as CPU usage, memory utilization, disk space, and network statistics. By automating the collection and processing of these metrics, shell scripts facilitate system monitoring and generate valuable insights for analysis.

8. **Software Deployment and Configuration**: Shell scripts play a vital role in software deployment and configuration management. They can automate the installation and setup of software packages, perform version checks, and configure application settings. Shell scripts are commonly used in continuous integration and deployment (CI/CD) pipelines to facilitate the deployment process.

9. **Network Operations**: Shell scripting enables network operations such as remote server management, file transfers, network monitoring, and automated interactions with network devices. By leveraging tools like SSH, SCP, and network monitoring utilities, shell scripts provide a means to automate and streamline network-related tasks.

10. **Custom Tools and Utilities**: Shell scripting empowers users to develop custom tools and utilities tailored to their specific needs. By combining shell commands, logic, and external programs, users can create specialized tools for tasks not covered by existing software. These custom scripts enhance productivity and enable users to solve unique problems efficiently.

The benefits and use cases of shell scripting are diverse and adaptable. Its simplicity, flexibility, and integration capabilities make it an invaluable tool for automating tasks, managing systems, processing data, and customizing the shell environment. By harnessing the power of shell scripting, users can optimize their workflows, increase efficiency, and accomplish tasks with ease.

1.3 Understanding the Bash Shell

The Bash shell (Bourne Again SHell) is a widely used shell and scripting language in the Unix and Linux environments. It is the default shell for most Linux distributions and macOS, offering a powerful and feature-rich command-line interface. Understanding the Bash shell is crucial for effective shell scripting. Let's delve into its key characteristics and functionalities:

1. **Command-Line Interpreter**: The Bash shell serves as a command-line interpreter, accepting and executing commands entered by the user. It provides a prompt where commands can be entered interactively or executed from a script file. The shell reads commands, interprets them, and communicates with the operating system to perform the requested actions.

2. **Interactive Shell**: Bash allows users to interactively enter commands, providing immediate feedback and results. This interactive mode is highly useful for executing ad-hoc commands, exploring the system, and performing quick tasks without the need for a script.

3. **Scripting Language**: Bash incorporates scripting capabilities, enabling users to write and execute shell scripts. The scripting language supports variables, control structures (such as loops and conditional statements), functions, command substitution, and input/output redirection. This scripting functionality empowers users to automate tasks and create complex sequences of commands.

4. **Environment Customization**: Bash provides extensive customization options to tailor the shell environment according to individual preferences. Users can define aliases (shortcuts for commands), environment variables, shell options, and shell functions to enhance productivity and streamline workflows. The .bashrc or .bash_profile files are commonly used to store these customizations.

5. **Command History**: Bash maintains a command history, allowing users to recall and re-execute previously entered commands easily. This history feature is accessible using arrow keys or by searching through the history using the Ctrl+R shortcut. Command history can be a valuable asset for reusing commands, saving time, and avoiding repetitive typing.

6. **Tab Completion**: Bash offers tab completion, a convenient feature that assists users in typing commands, filenames, and paths. By pressing the Tab key, Bash intelligently completes partially entered commands or suggests available options based on the context. This feature improves efficiency and reduces typing errors.

7. **Job Control**: Bash provides job control mechanisms for managing multiple processes running in the shell. Users can start processes in the foreground or background, switch between them,

suspend them, and resume their execution. Job control is particularly useful when working with long-running or parallel tasks.

8. **Redirection and Pipes**: Bash supports input/output redirection and pipes, enabling data flow manipulation between commands. Redirection allows the capture of command output into files or the redirection of input from files. Pipes enable the chaining of multiple commands, where the output of one command serves as input to the next, creating powerful data processing pipelines.

9. **Command Substitution**: Bash facilitates command substitution, a mechanism to capture the output of a command and use it as part of another command or assignment. Command substitution is denoted by $() or backticks ( ). This feature enables dynamic script execution and integration of command output into variable assignments or command parameters.

10. **Extensive Command-Line Utilities**: Bash integrates with a vast array of command-line utilities, tools, and programs available in Unix-like systems. These utilities provide additional functionality for text processing, file manipulation, system administration, networking, and more. By leveraging these utilities, users can extend the capabilities of their shell scripts.

Understanding the features and functionalities of the Bash shell is fundamental to becoming proficient in shell scripting. Whether it's executing commands interactively, writing shell scripts, customizing the shell environment, or utilizing advanced features like job control and command substitution, a solid understanding of Bash empowers users to harness the full potential of the command-line interface.

1.4 Overview of the Bash Scripting Language

The Bash scripting language is a powerful tool for automating tasks, creating scripts, and enhancing the functionality of the Bash shell. It combines the features of a command-line interpreter with the flexibility of a scripting language, providing a robust environment for writing shell scripts. Let's explore the key components and constructs of the Bash scripting language:

1. **Variables**: Bash allows the declaration and usage of variables to store data. Variables are created by assigning values to them, and they can store various types of data such as strings, numbers, or arrays. Variables are referenced using the $ symbol, such as $variable_name. Bash also provides special variables, like $0 (script name) and $1, $2, etc. (command-line arguments).

2. **Control Structures**: Bash supports control structures for conditional execution and loop control. Conditional statements like if, elif, and else allow for branching based on specific conditions. Loops such as for, while, and until enable repetitive execution of commands until a condition is met.

3. **Functions**: Bash allows the creation of functions to group a set of commands into a reusable block. Functions enhance code modularity and maintainability. They can accept arguments, process data, and return values. Functions are defined using the function keyword or simply by using the function name followed by parentheses.

4. **Command Substitution**: Bash supports command substitution, which allows the output of a command to replace the command itself within a command or assignment. Command substitution can be performed using the $() syntax or the backtick ( ) symbol. This feature facilitates dynamic script execution and incorporating command output into scripts.

5. **Input and Output**: Bash provides mechanisms for input and output operations within scripts. Standard input (stdin), standard output (stdout), and standard error (stderr) streams can be manipulated using redirection operators (<, >, >>, etc.) to read from or write to files. Additionally, the echo command is commonly used to display output, and the read

command allows script interaction by reading user input.

6. **String Manipulation**: Bash offers extensive capabilities for string manipulation. It supports concatenation, slicing, length determination, substitution, and pattern matching using wildcard characters (*, ?, etc.). String manipulation is crucial for text processing, data parsing, and generating formatted output.

7. **File Operations**: Bash provides a wide range of operations for file handling. It allows file creation, deletion, copying, moving, and renaming. It also supports file permission management, directory navigation, and file attribute retrieval. These file operations enable efficient management and manipulation of files and directories within scripts.

8. **Error Handling**: Bash facilitates error handling within scripts. It supports capturing and processing errors using conditional statements and exit codes. The exit command can be used to terminate the script and return an exit code, enabling effective error management and script behavior control.

9. **Arithmetic Operations**: Bash allows arithmetic operations, including addition, subtraction, multiplication, division, and modulus. These operations can be performed using the $(( )) syntax or the let command. Arithmetic operations are valuable

when performing calculations or implementing mathematical logic within scripts.

10. **External Program Integration**: Bash seamlessly integrates with external programs and utilities. It allows the execution of system commands, invocation of external programs, and processing of their output. This integration enables the utilization of existing tools and utilities to extend the functionality of shell scripts.

The Bash scripting language combines these components and constructs to create powerful and flexible shell scripts. By leveraging variables, control structures, functions, command substitution, input/output operations, string manipulation, file operations, error handling, arithmetic operations, and external program integration, users can develop robust and efficient scripts to automate tasks, solve problems, and streamline operations within the Bash shell environment.

Chapter 2: Getting Started with Bash

Welcome to the world of Bash scripting! In this chapter, we'll help you take your first steps towards becoming a proficient scripter. We'll begin by guiding you through the process of installing Bash and launching the shell. You'll learn how to navigate the shell environment, execute basic commands, and gain familiarity with the command-line interface.

Whether you're a complete beginner or have some experience with the command line, this chapter will provide you with the essential knowledge to get started with Bash. So, let's embark on this journey together and unlock the power of Bash scripting!

2.1 Installing Bash

Installing Bash is a straightforward process that can be done on various operating systems. Here are the installation instructions for different platforms:

1. Linux:

Most Linux distributions come pre-installed with Bash. However, if you need to install it manually or ensure you have the latest version, you can use the package manager specific to your distribution. Here are a few examples:

Ubuntu/Debian: Open the terminal and run the following command:

sudo apt-get install bash

CentOS/Fedora: Open the terminal and run the following command:

sudo yum install bash

Arch Linux: Open the terminal and run the following command:

sudo pacman -S bash

2. macOS:

Bash is the default shell in macOS. However, older versions of macOS use Bash 3, while newer versions (macOS Catalina and later) use Zsh as the default shell. If you prefer to use Bash, you can install the latest version using package managers such as Homebrew or MacPorts.

Homebrew: Open the terminal and run the following command to install Homebrew if you haven't already:

/bin/bash -c "$(curl -fsSL https://raw.githubusercontent.com/Homebrew/install/HEAD/install.sh)"

Then, install Bash by running:

brew install bash

MacPorts: Open the terminal and run the following command to install MacPorts if you haven't already:

sudo port selfupdate

Then, install Bash by running:

sudo port install bash

3. Windows:

Windows doesn't come with Bash installed by default. However, you can install it by using the Windows Subsystem for Linux (WSL) feature, which provides a Linux environment on Windows.

WSL1: Open the Microsoft Store and search for "Ubuntu" or the Linux distribution of your choice. Install the distribution, launch it, and follow the setup instructions to create a new user and password. Bash will be available within the Linux distribution.

WSL2: Follow the instructions provided by Microsoft to enable and install WSL2 on your Windows system. Once installed, open the Microsoft Store and search for a Linux distribution like "Ubuntu." Install the distribution, launch it, and complete the setup. Bash will be available within the Linux distribution.

4. Other Platforms:

For other platforms, including BSD variants and Unix-like systems, refer to the specific package manager or the official documentation for installation instructions.

After installing Bash, you can open a terminal or command prompt and type bash to start a Bash session. You can also check the version of Bash installed by running bash --version. With Bash successfully installed, you're ready to start using it for shell scripting and interactive command-line operations.

2.2 Launching the Bash Shell

Launching the Bash shell allows you to access the command-line interface and start executing commands or running Bash scripts. The method of launching the Bash shell may vary depending on the operating system you are using. Here are the common ways to launch the Bash shell on different platforms:

1. Linux:

On Linux, launching the Bash shell is typically done through a terminal emulator. Here's how you can do it:

Open the terminal emulator of your choice. It is usually found in the applications menu or can be launched using a keyboard shortcut (e.g., Ctrl+Alt+T).

The terminal emulator will open a new window, displaying the command-line prompt. By default, it will start with the Bash shell.

2. macOS:

On macOS, you can launch the Bash shell using the built-in Terminal application. Here's how:

Open the Finder.

Go to "Applications" > "Utilities" and double-click on "Terminal".

The Terminal application will open, providing you with a new terminal window running the Bash shell.

Alternatively, if you have installed an updated version of Bash using package managers like Homebrew or

MacPorts, you can launch it by typing bash in the terminal.

3. Windows:

On Windows, you can launch the Bash shell if you have Windows Subsystem for Linux (WSL) installed. Here's how:

Open the Start menu and search for the Linux distribution you have installed (e.g., Ubuntu, Debian).

Click on the distribution to launch it.

The distribution's terminal window will open, providing you with access to the Bash shell.

If you haven't installed WSL or a Linux distribution, you can consider using a terminal emulator such as Git Bash, Cygwin, or Windows Terminal, which provide a Bash-like environment on Windows.

4. Other Platforms:

For other platforms, including BSD variants and Unix-like systems, launching the Bash shell is generally done through a terminal emulator or command prompt specific to that platform. Refer to the documentation or search for instructions related to the specific operating system you are using.

Once you have launched the Bash shell, you will see a command-line prompt where you can start typing commands or executing Bash scripts. You can enter commands interactively, run shell scripts using the bash command followed by the script name, or use other Bash features and functionalities to accomplish various tasks within the shell environment.

Remember to consult the Bash documentation or access online resources for more information on the specific capabilities and features available within the Bash shell.

2.3 Navigating the Shell Environment

Once you have launched the Bash shell, navigating the shell environment is essential for effective command-line operations. Here are some fundamental navigation commands to help you move around the shell:

1. **Present Working Directory (pwd):** To know your current location within the directory structure, use the pwd command. It displays the absolute path of the directory you are currently in.

2. **Listing Files and Directories (ls):** Use the ls command to list the contents of a directory. By default, it shows the files and directories in the current

directory. You can also provide a specific path to list the contents of a different directory.

Common options for ls:

- -l: Long format listing with detailed information.
- -a: Include hidden files and directories starting with a dot (.).
- -h: Print file sizes in human-readable format (e.g., kilobytes, megabytes).

3. **Changing Directories (cd):** The cd command allows you to change your current working directory. You can specify the directory name or provide a path to navigate to a specific directory.

Common cd usage:

- cd directory_name: Change to the specified directory.
- cd ..: Move up one level to the parent directory.
- cd /: Move to the root directory.
- cd ~: Move to the home directory.

4. **Creating Directories (mkdir):** To create a new directory, use the mkdir command followed by the directory name. You can also provide a path to create directories within a specific location.

Example: mkdir new_directory creates a directory named "new_directory" in the current location.

5. **Removing Files and Directories (rm):** The rm command is used to delete files and directories.

To delete a file: rm file_name

To delete an empty directory: rmdir directory_name

To delete a directory and its contents recursively: rm -r directory_name

6. **Moving or Renaming Files and Directories (mv):** The mv command is used to move or rename files and directories.

To move a file or directory to a new location: mv source destination

To rename a file or directory: mv old_name new_name

7. **Copying Files and Directories (cp):** The cp command allows you to copy files and directories.

To copy a file to a new location: cp source destination

To copy a directory and its contents recursively: cp -r source_dir destination_dir

8. **Tab Completion**: Bash provides tab completion, which allows you to quickly complete file and directory

names by pressing the Tab key. It saves time and helps avoid typos while navigating the shell environment.

These basic navigation commands will help you explore the directory structure, create and remove directories, and move or rename files and directories within the shell environment. Experiment with these commands to become familiar with navigating the shell and effectively managing your files and directories.

2.4 Basic Shell Commands

The Bash shell provides a wide range of basic commands that allow you to perform various operations within the shell environment. Here are some essential shell commands to get you started:

1. **Clear the Screen (clear):** The clear command clears the terminal screen, giving you a clean slate to work with.

2. **Print Working Directory (pwd):** The pwd command displays the absolute path of the current working directory.

3. **List Files and Directories (ls):** The ls command lists the contents of a directory.

Common options for ls:

- -l: Long format listing with detailed information.
- -a: Include hidden files and directories starting with a dot (.).
- -h: Print file sizes in human-readable format (e.g., kilobytes, megabytes).

4. **Change Directory (cd):** The cd command allows you to change the current working directory.

Common cd usage:

- cd directory_name: Change to the specified directory.
- cd ..: Move up one level to the parent directory.
- cd /: Move to the root directory.
- cd ~: Move to the home directory.

5. **Make Directory (mkdir):** The mkdir command is used to create a new directory.

Example: mkdir new_directory creates a directory named "new_directory" in the current location.

6. **Remove Files and Directories (rm):** The rm command deletes files and directories.

- To delete a file: rm file_name
- To delete an empty directory: rmdir directory_name

- To delete a directory and its contents recursively: rm -r directory_name

7. **Copy Files and Directories (cp):** The cp command allows you to copy files and directories.

    - To copy a file to a new location: cp source destination
    - To copy a directory and its contents recursively: cp -r source_dir destination_dir

8. **Move or Rename Files and Directories (mv):** The mv command is used to move or rename files and directories.

To move a file or directory to a new location: mv source destination
To rename a file or directory: mv old_name new_name

9. **View File Contents (cat, less, head, tail):** These commands allow you to view the contents of a file.

    - cat file_name: Display the entire contents of a file.
    - less file_name: View the contents of a file interactively, allowing scrolling and searching.
    - head file_name: Display the first few lines of a file.
    - tail file_name: Display the last few lines of a file.

10. **Text Editor (nano, vi/vim):** Bash includes text editors like nano and vi (or vim) that allow you to create and edit text files directly from the command line.

- nano file_name: Open the file in the nano text editor.
- vi file_name or vim file_name: Open the file in the vi or vim text editor.

These basic shell commands provide essential functionality for file and directory manipulation, file viewing, and text editing within the Bash shell environment. As you become more comfortable with these commands, you can explore additional options and advanced features to enhance your shell experience.

Chapter 3: Setting Up Your Shell Environment

A well-configured shell environment is the key to efficient and enjoyable shell scripting. In this chapter, we'll guide you through the process of setting up your shell environment to suit your needs. You'll learn how to customize your shell prompt, configure shell preferences, and explore the various options available to tailor your experience.

Whether you're a perfectionist seeking a personalized environment or a pragmatic scripter looking for optimal settings, this chapter will equip you with the knowledge and tools to create a comfortable and productive shell environment. Get ready to unleash the full potential of your shell and elevate your scripting experience to new heights!

3.1 Configuring Shell Preferences

Configuring your shell preferences allows you to customize the behavior and appearance of the Bash shell to suit your needs and preferences. Here are some common ways to configure your shell preferences:

1. Shell Configuration Files:

The Bash shell uses configuration files to set up environment variables, define aliases, and specify custom shell settings. The two primary configuration files are:

~/.bashrc: This file is executed each time you start an interactive Bash shell. You can add customizations, such as defining aliases or setting environment variables, to this file.

~/.bash_profile (or ~/.bash_login): This file is executed when you log in to your account. It is typically used to set up environment variables and perform initialization tasks that should only happen once at login.

You can edit these files using a text editor like nano or vi. For example, to edit ~/.bashrc, run nano ~/.bashrc. Make the desired changes, save the file, and restart your shell for the changes to take effect.

2. Environment Variables:

Environment variables are global variables that define various aspects of the shell environment. They can control behaviors, store configuration values, and provide information to programs and scripts. Some commonly used environment variables include:

- **PATH**: Specifies the directories where the shell looks for executable files.
- **PS1**: Defines the prompt string that appears before each command.
- **HOME**: Points to the current user's home directory.
- **LANG**: Determines the language and localization settings.

You can view and modify environment variables using the printenv command to display their current values, and the export command to set or modify their values. For example, export PATH=$PATH:/new/directory adds a new directory to the PATH variable.

3. Aliases:

Aliases are shortcuts for frequently used commands or command sequences. They help you save time and avoid typing long commands repeatedly. You can define aliases in your shell configuration files (~/.bashrc or ~/.bash_profile) using the alias command. For example:

alias ll='ls -alF': Defines ll as an alias for the ls -alF command, which lists all files and directories in a detailed format.

After defining an alias, it becomes available for immediate use in your shell session or in subsequent sessions after restarting the shell.

4. Prompt Customization:

You can customize the appearance of your shell prompt using special escape sequences. The prompt can display information such as the username, hostname, current directory, and more. The customization is done by modifying the PS1 environment variable. For example:

export PS1="\u@\h:\w $ ": Sets the prompt to display the username, hostname, and current working directory.

You can experiment with different escape sequences and formatting options to create a personalized prompt.

5. Terminal Emulator Preferences:

If you're using a graphical terminal emulator, it may have its own preferences and settings that you can customize. These settings can include font styles, colors, cursor behavior, and more. Access the preferences or settings menu of your terminal emulator to explore and modify these options.

Remember to save your changes in the relevant configuration files and restart your shell to apply the modifications.

By configuring your shell preferences, you can make your shell environment more efficient, convenient, and visually appealing. Experiment with different settings and options to create a personalized and productive shell experience.

3.2 Customizing the Shell Prompt

The shell prompt is the text displayed before each command in the Bash shell. Customizing the prompt allows you to personalize its appearance and include helpful information. Here are some ways to customize the shell prompt:

1. Using Escape Sequences:

Escape sequences are special character sequences that are interpreted by the shell and replaced with specific values. You can use escape sequences to include dynamic information in your prompt. Here are some commonly used escape sequences:

- \u: Username of the current user.
- \h: Hostname of the system.
- \w: Current working directory.
- \n: Newline.
- \t: Current time in 24-hour format.
- \s: Name of the shell.

For example, setting the PS1 variable in your shell configuration file (~/.bashrc or ~/.bash_profile) to export PS1="\u@\h:\w $ " will result in a prompt that displays the username, hostname, and current working directory.

2. Customizing Colors:

You can use ANSI color codes to add colors to your prompt. ANSI color codes are special character sequences that instruct the terminal to display text in different colors. Here's an example of setting a colored prompt:

export PS1="\[\e[32m\]\u@\h:\w $ \[\e[0m\]": This sets the prompt with the username and hostname in green color.

In the example, \[\e[32m\] sets the color to green, and \[\e[0m\] resets the color to the default.

3. Displaying Git Branch:

If you work with Git repositories, you can include the current Git branch in your prompt to provide quick information about the repository status. Several tools and scripts are available to achieve this, such as the popular "git-prompt" script. You can find instructions for integrating such scripts into your prompt in the respective documentation.

4. Prompt Variables:

Bash provides additional variables that allow you to customize the prompt further. Some commonly used variables include:

- **PS1**: The primary prompt string.
- **PS2**: The secondary prompt string, displayed when a command requires additional input (e.g., multiline commands).
- **PS3**: The prompt string for the select command.
- **PS4**: The prompt string for tracing shell scripts (set -x).

By modifying these variables, you can create different prompt styles and behaviors for various scenarios.

Remember to save your changes to the shell configuration file and restart your shell for the modifications to take effect.

Customizing the shell prompt enhances the user experience by providing personalized information and visual cues. Experiment with different escape sequences, colors, and prompt variables to create a prompt that suits your preferences and improves your workflow.

3.3 Working with Shell Configuration Files

Shell configuration files play a crucial role in customizing and setting up your shell environment. They allow you to define environment variables, set aliases, and specify various settings. In this section, we'll explore some common tasks related to working with shell configuration files, such as ~/.bashrc and ~/.bash_profile.

1. Opening the Configuration Files:

To work with the shell configuration files, you'll need to open them in a text editor. Here are some commonly used editors:

nano: Run nano ~/.bashrc or nano ~/.bash_profile to open the respective file in the nano text editor.

vi/vim: Run vi ~/.bashrc or vi ~/.bash_profile to open the respective file in the vi or vim text editor.

Choose the editor you're most comfortable with and open the desired configuration file for editing.

2. Adding Environment Variables:

Environment variables define various aspects of your shell environment. To add or modify environment variables, follow these steps:

1. Open the configuration file in your preferred text editor.
2. Locate the section where you want to add the environment variable or find an existing variable to modify.
3. Add or modify the variable in the following format: export VARIABLE_NAME=value. For example, export PATH=$PATH:/usr/local/bin adds /usr/local/bin to the existing PATH variable.
4. Save the file after making the changes.

Remember to reload the configuration by restarting the shell or running source ~/.bashrc (or source ~/.bash_profile) to apply the changes immediately.

3. Defining Aliases:

Aliases are shortcuts for frequently used commands or command sequences. To define aliases in your configuration files, follow these steps:

1. Open the configuration file in your preferred text editor.
2. Locate the section where you want to add the alias or find an existing alias to modify.

3. Add or modify the alias using the following format: alias ALIAS_NAME='command'. For example, alias ll='ls -alF' defines ll as an alias for the ls -alF command.
4. Save the file after making the changes.

Remember to reload the configuration by restarting the shell or running source ~/.bashrc (or source ~/.bash_profile) to make the aliases available immediately.

4. Customizing the Prompt:

To customize your shell prompt, modify the PS1 variable in your configuration file. Here's an example:

1. export PS1="\u@\h:\w $ ": Sets the prompt to display the username, hostname, and current working directory.
2. Modify the PS1 variable according to your desired prompt format. Save the file and reload the configuration to apply the changes.

5. Reloading the Configuration:

After making changes to the configuration file, you need to reload the configuration to apply the modifications. There are two ways to achieve this:

1. **Restart the shell**: Close the terminal window and open a new one. The changes will be applied when the new shell starts.
2. **Use the source command**: Run source ~/.bashrc (or source ~/.bash_profile) to reload the configuration immediately without restarting the shell.

By following these steps, you can work effectively with shell configuration files, add or modify environment variables, define aliases, and customize the prompt. These files provide a powerful way to tailor your shell environment to your specific needs and preferences.

3.4 Managing Environment Variables

Environment variables play a crucial role in configuring your shell environment. They define various settings, paths, and options that determine how your shell and other programs behave. In this section, we'll explore how to manage environment variables effectively.

1. Viewing Environment Variables:

To view the current environment variables in your shell, you can use the printenv command. Running printenv without any arguments will display a list of all environment variables and their values.

If you want to view a specific environment variable, use the following syntax: printenv VARIABLE_NAME. For example, printenv PATH will display the value of the PATH variable.

2. Setting Environment Variables:

To set or modify an environment variable, you can use the export command. The general syntax is export VARIABLE_NAME=value.

For example, to set the EDITOR variable to nano, you would run: export EDITOR=nano. This sets the EDITOR variable to nano for the current shell session.

If you want the variable to persist across multiple shell sessions, you'll need to add the export command to your shell configuration file (~/.bashrc or ~/.bash_profile). This ensures that the variable is set every time you start a new shell session.

3. Modifying Environment Variables:

To modify the value of an existing environment variable, you can simply assign a new value to it. For example, to add a directory to the PATH variable, you would use the following syntax: export PATH=$PATH:/new/directory.

Note that when modifying the PATH variable, it's essential to include the existing value ($PATH) to avoid overwriting it entirely. By appending :/new/directory to $PATH, you add the new directory to the existing PATH value.

4. Removing Environment Variables:

To remove an environment variable, you can use the unset command followed by the variable name. For example, to remove the EDITOR variable, run: unset EDITOR.

After running this command, the EDITOR variable will no longer be available in your shell session.

5. Temporarily Setting Environment Variables:

If you need to set an environment variable temporarily for a specific command or script, you can use the following syntax:

VARIABLE_NAME=value command

For example, to set the EDITOR variable to nano only for the duration of running a script called myscript.sh, you would run: EDITOR=nano ./myscript.sh.

This technique allows you to override or set environment variables on a per-command basis without permanently modifying your shell configuration.

By effectively managing environment variables, you can configure your shell environment to meet your specific needs. Whether it's setting important paths, defining default options, or customizing the behavior of your shell, environment variables provide a flexible and powerful way to tailor your environment.

Chapter 4: Basic Bash Commands and Syntax

In this chapter, we will delve into the fundamental building blocks of Bash scripting: commands and syntax. You will learn how to execute commands in the Bash shell, explore various command-line options and arguments, and understand the syntax conventions that govern the structure of your scripts.

We will cover essential concepts such as input/output redirection, pipelines, and command substitution, allowing you to manipulate and process data effectively. By mastering these basic Bash commands and syntax, you will gain the confidence to write simple yet powerful scripts to automate your tasks.

Whether you're a beginner or have some experience with Bash, this chapter will provide you with a solid foundation in executing commands and understanding the syntax of the Bash scripting language. Get ready to unlock the true potential of your scripts with the fundamental tools of Bash!

4.1 Executing Commands in the Shell

Executing commands is one of the fundamental tasks in the shell environment. Whether it's running built-in shell commands or invoking external programs, knowing how to execute commands effectively is essential. In this section, we'll explore different ways to execute commands in the shell.

1. Running Shell Commands:

The shell provides a wide range of built-in commands that perform various operations. To run a shell command, simply type the command and press Enter. For example, running ls lists the files and directories in the current directory.

You can pass arguments to a command by providing them after the command name. For example, ls -l lists the files and directories in a long format.

2. Executing External Programs:

In addition to built-in shell commands, you can execute external programs or scripts from the shell. To execute an external program, provide the program's name as the command.

For example, to run the python interpreter, you would type python and press Enter. This launches the Python interpreter, allowing you to interact with the Python environment.

You can provide command-line arguments to external programs in the same way as shell commands by specifying them after the program name. For example, python script.py runs the Python script named script.py.

3. Command Substitution:

Command substitution allows you to capture the output of a command and use it as part of another command or assign it to a variable. There are two syntaxes for command substitution:

- **Using Backticks**: Enclose the command within backticks (`command`). For example, to assign the output of the date command to a variable named current_date, you would use: current_date=date``.
- **Using Dollar Parentheses**: Enclose the command within dollar parentheses ($(command)). For example, the same command substitution can be written as: current_date=$(date).

Command substitution is useful when you want to use the output of one command as an argument to another or store it for later use.

4. Running Commands in the Background:

By default, commands execute in the foreground, meaning the shell waits for the command to complete before executing the next command. However, you can run commands in the background, allowing you to continue working in the shell while the command runs.

To run a command in the background, append an ampersand (&) at the end of the command. For example, python script.py & runs the Python script in the background.

5. Redirecting Input and Output:

You can redirect the input and output of commands to or from files using redirection operators.

- **Input Redirection (<):** Reads input from a file instead of the standard input. For example, sort < input.txt reads the contents of input.txt as input for the sort command.
- **Output Redirection (>):** Redirects the output of a command to a file instead of the standard output. For example, ls > output.txt writes the output of the ls command to the file output.txt.

These are just a few examples of how you can execute commands in the shell. Mastering command execution is crucial for working effectively in the shell environment, whether it's running shell commands, executing external programs, capturing command output, or redirecting input and output. Practice these techniques to become proficient in executing commands and harness the power of the shell.

4.2 Command-Line Options and Arguments

Command-line options and arguments provide a flexible way to customize the behavior of commands and programs in the shell. They allow you to specify additional parameters, toggle certain features, or provide input data to the command. In this section, we'll explore command-line options and arguments and how to use them effectively.

1. Command-Line Options:

Command-line options, also known as flags or switches, modify the behavior of a command or program. They are typically preceded by a hyphen (-) or a double hyphen (--). Here are some common ways to use command-line options:

- **Single-Character Options**: Single-character options are typically preceded by a single hyphen. For example, -l is a single-character option that might enable a long listing format in a command like ls -l.
- **Combined Options**: You can combine multiple single-character options after a single hyphen. For example, ls -la combines the -l and -a options to list files in long format, including hidden files.

- **Long Options**: Long options are more descriptive and are preceded by a double hyphen. For example, --recursive is a long option that might enable recursive directory traversal in a command like grep --recursive.

The availability and usage of command-line options depend on the specific command or program you are using. Refer to the documentation or help page of the command to understand the available options and their meanings.

2. Command-Line Arguments:

Command-line arguments are additional pieces of information that you provide to a command or program. They typically come after the command and options. Here are a few examples:

- **grep pattern file.txt**: In this command, pattern is an argument representing the pattern to search for, and file.txt is an argument representing the file to search within.
- **cp file1.txt file2.txt directory**: In this command, file1.txt, file2.txt, and directory are arguments representing the source file, destination file, and destination directory, respectively.

The interpretation and usage of command-line arguments depend on the specific command or program. Some commands may require a certain number of arguments or specific formats for the arguments. Refer to the command's documentation or help page for guidance on using arguments correctly.

3. Options vs. Arguments:

It's important to understand the distinction between command-line options and arguments. Options modify the behavior of a command or program, while arguments provide additional information or inputs to the command. Options are typically preceded by a hyphen or double hyphen, while arguments are usually provided after the command and options.

For example, in the command ls -l file.txt, -l is an option that enables the long listing format, while file.txt is an argument representing the file to list.

4. Help and Usage Information:

Most commands and programs provide a way to display their usage information, including available options and argument formats. You can usually access this information by using the --help option. For example, ls --help displays the usage information for the ls command.

Reviewing the help information can guide you in understanding the available options and how to provide arguments correctly.

By understanding command-line options and arguments, you gain greater control over the behavior of commands and programs in the shell. Take advantage of available options and provide appropriate arguments to tailor command execution according to your requirements.

4.3 Redirecting Input and Output

Redirecting input and output in the shell allows you to control where the input comes from and where the output goes. This powerful feature enables you to manipulate data, save command output to files, and automate processes. In this section, we'll explore various techniques for redirecting input and output in the shell.

1. Output Redirection (>):

The > operator redirects the output of a command to a file instead of displaying it on the terminal. It creates or overwrites the contents of the file with the command output. Here's an example:

command > output.txt

This command runs command and redirects its output to the file output.txt. If the file already exists, it will be overwritten. If it doesn't exist, a new file will be created.

2. Appending Output (>>):

The >> operator appends the output of a command to the end of a file, preserving its existing contents. If the file doesn't exist, it will be created. Here's an example:

command >> output.txt

This command runs command and appends its output to the file output.txt.

3. Input Redirection (<):

The < operator redirects the input of a command from a file instead of receiving it from the keyboard. Here's an example:

command < input.txt

This command runs command and takes its input from the file input.txt rather than from the keyboard.

4. Piping Output (|):

Piping allows you to take the output of one command and use it as the input for another command. The | symbol connects the output of the preceding command to the input of the following command. Here's an example:

command1 | command2

This command runs command1 and pipes its output to command2 as input. command2 will process the data received from command1.

Piping is a powerful mechanism for chaining commands together and performing complex operations by combining the functionality of multiple commands.

5. Discarding Output (>/dev/null):

If you want to discard the output of a command and prevent it from being displayed on the terminal or saved to a file, you can redirect it to the special file /dev/null. Here's an example:

command > /dev/null

This command runs command and redirects its output to /dev/null, effectively discarding it.

Redirecting output to /dev/null is useful when you don't need to see the output but still want the command to execute.

6. Redirecting Standard Error (2>):

By default, the output of a command is sent to the standard output (stdout). However, error messages or diagnostic information are often sent to the standard error (stderr). To redirect the standard error, you can use the 2> operator. Here's an example:

command 2> error.txt

This command runs command and redirects its error messages to the file error.txt. It captures the stderr output separately from the stdout output.

Redirecting standard error allows you to isolate and handle error messages separately from normal output.

By mastering input and output redirection, you gain greater control over how data flows in and out of commands. You can store output in files, combine commands using piping, discard unnecessary output, and manage error messages effectively. These techniques enhance your productivity and allow you to automate tasks efficiently in the shell.

4.4 Pipelines and Filters

Pipelines and filters are powerful concepts in shell scripting that allow you to connect multiple commands together to perform complex data manipulation and processing tasks. By combining commands using pipelines, you can create a chain of data flow where the output of one command becomes the input for the next. In this section, we'll explore pipelines and filters in more detail.

1. Pipelines (|):

The pipeline operator (|) connects the output of one command to the input of another command. It enables you to create a seamless flow of data between commands, allowing you to perform successive operations on the data. Here's an example:

command1 | command2

This command runs command1 and pipes its output as input to command2. The output of command1 is processed by command2, and the result can be further piped to additional commands if needed.

Pipelines are particularly useful when you want to combine the functionality of multiple commands to achieve a specific task or process large amounts of data efficiently.

2. Filters:

Filters are commands that accept input, perform a specific operation on it, and produce output. They are designed to process and transform data in a meaningful way. Filters are commonly used in pipelines to perform various tasks, such as searching, sorting, formatting, and filtering data.

Here are some commonly used filters:

- **grep**: Searches for lines in the input that match a specific pattern.
- **sort**: Sorts the input in a specified order, such as alphabetically or numerically.
- **sed**: Performs text transformations based on patterns and rules.
- **awk**: Processes and manipulates text data using patterns and actions.
- **cut**: Extracts specific fields or columns from the input.
- **head and tail**: Selects the top or bottom lines from the input, respectively.

By combining filters in a pipeline, you can create powerful data processing workflows. For example, you can search for specific lines using grep, sort the results using sort, and then extract specific fields using cut.

3. Examples:

Let's look at a couple of examples to illustrate the use of pipelines and filters:

Example 1:

ls -l | grep ".txt" | sort -r | head -n 5

In this example, the ls -l command lists the files and directories in long format. The output is then piped to grep to filter only the lines containing the ".txt" pattern. The filtered output is further piped to sort -r to sort the lines in reverse order. Finally, head -n 5 selects the top 5 lines from the sorted output.

Example 2:

cat data.txt | awk '{print $2}' | sort | uniq -c

In this example, the cat data.txt command reads the contents of the file "data.txt". The output is piped to awk to extract the second field from each line. The extracted values are then piped to sort to sort them alphabetically. Finally, uniq -c counts the occurrences of each unique value in the sorted output.

These examples demonstrate how pipelines and filters can be combined to perform powerful data processing operations, enabling you to extract valuable insights, transform data, and automate tasks efficiently.

By understanding pipelines and utilizing filters effectively, you can leverage the full potential of the shell environment to process and manipulate data in a seamless and efficient manner.

4.5 Command Substitution

Command substitution is a shell feature that allows you to capture the output of a command and use it as part of another command or store it in a variable. It provides a convenient way to incorporate the results of one command into another command or perform further operations on the captured output. In this section, we'll explore command substitution and its various forms.

1. Syntax:

Command substitution has two main forms in the shell: using backticks (` `` `) or using the $() syntax. Here's the general syntax:

Backticks (` `` `) form:

output=`command`

$() form:

output=$(command)

In both forms, the command is executed, and its output is captured and assigned to the output variable. You can then use the output variable in subsequent commands or operations.

2. Examples:

Let's look at a few examples to illustrate the use of command substitution:

Example 1: Capturing command output:

current_date=$(date +%Y-%m-%d)
echo "Today's date is: $current_date"

In this example, the date +%Y-%m-%d command retrieves the current date in the format "YYYY-MM-DD". The output of the command is captured using command substitution and assigned to the current_date variable. The variable is then used in the echo command to display the current date.

Example 2: Using command output in a command:

file_count=$(ls | wc -l)

echo "Number of files in the directory: $file_count"

In this example, the ls command lists the files in the current directory. The output is piped to the wc -l command, which counts the number of lines. The count is captured using command substitution and stored in the file_count variable. The variable is then used in the echo command to display the number of files in the directory.

65

Example 3: Command substitution in a command argument:

echo "The current working directory is: $(pwd)"

In this example, the pwd command prints the current working directory. The output is directly substituted within the echo command, allowing the current working directory to be displayed as part of the message.

Command substitution provides a flexible way to incorporate the output of one command into another command or store it in a variable for further processing. It allows you to dynamically generate command arguments, build complex commands, and automate tasks based on the results of other commands.

Remember to choose the appropriate command substitution syntax (``` or $()) based on your preference or compatibility with the shell environment you are using.

By leveraging command substitution effectively, you can enhance the functionality and automation capabilities of your shell scripts, making them more powerful and efficient.

Chapter 5: Variables and Data Types in Bash

Variables are the backbone of any scripting language, and Bash is no exception. In this chapter, we will explore the world of variables in Bash and understand how they enable us to store and manipulate data.

We will start by learning about variable declaration and assignment, understanding the rules for naming variables and assigning values to them. You will discover the various data types available in Bash, such as strings, numbers, and arrays, and how to work with each of them effectively.

Moreover, we will delve into the concepts of variable scope and lifetime, exploring how variables behave within different contexts and understanding their lifespan within scripts. You will gain insights into local and global variables and how to utilize them to your advantage.

By the end of this chapter, you will have a solid grasp of variable usage in Bash and be able to harness their power to create dynamic and interactive scripts. Get ready to unlock the potential of variables and take your Bash scripting skills to the next level!

5.1 Understanding Variables in Bash

Variables are an essential component of shell scripting, allowing you to store and manipulate data within your scripts. In Bash, variables are used to hold values such as text strings, numbers, and command outputs. Understanding how variables work is crucial for effective scripting. In this section, we'll explore variables in Bash and how to use them.

1. Variable Naming Convention:

In Bash, variable names are case-sensitive and can consist of letters, numbers, and underscores. However, they must start with a letter or an underscore. It's important to choose descriptive names that reflect the purpose of the variable. For example:

name="John"
age=25

2. Assigning Values to Variables:
To assign a value to a variable, use the assignment operator (=) without any spaces around it. Here's an example:

name="John"

In this case, the variable name is assigned the value "John".

3. Accessing Variable Values:

To access the value stored in a variable, precede the variable name with a dollar sign ($). Here's an example:

echo $name

This command prints the value of the name variable, which is "John".

4. Variable Types:

In Bash, variables are untyped, which means you can store any type of data in them. The type of a variable is determined by the context in which it is used. By default, variables are treated as strings unless explicitly converted or interpreted differently. However, you can also explicitly declare variables as integers using the declare or typeset command. For example:

declare -i age=25

In this case, the age variable is declared as an integer, and Bash will treat it as such, allowing you to perform arithmetic operations on it.

5. Modifying Variable Values:

To modify the value of a variable, simply assign a new value to it using the assignment operator (=). For example:

name="John"
name="Jane"

In this example, the name variable is first assigned the value "John" and then reassigned the value "Jane".

6. Command Substitution in Variables:

Variables can also store the output of commands using command substitution. Here's an example:

current_date=$(date +%Y-%m-%d)

In this case, the current_date variable is assigned the current date using the output of the date command.

7. Using Variables in Commands:

Variables can be used within commands by enclosing them in curly braces ({}) to separate them from surrounding text. Here's an example:

echo "My name is ${name}."

In this example, the value of the name variable is inserted into the echo command's output.

8. Deleting Variables:

To delete a variable and its value, use the unset command followed by the variable name. For example:

unset name

After this command, the name variable no longer exists.

Understanding variables and their usage is crucial for effective shell scripting. They enable you to store and manipulate data, interact with users, and make your scripts more dynamic and reusable. By mastering variables, you gain the ability to write powerful and flexible Bash scripts.

5.2 Declaring and Assigning Variables

In Bash scripting, declaring and assigning variables allows you to store and manipulate data within your scripts. By properly declaring and assigning variables, you can make your scripts more readable, maintainable, and flexible. In this section, we'll explore the process of declaring and assigning variables in Bash.

1. Variable Declaration:

In Bash, variable declaration is not mandatory. You can directly assign a value to a variable without explicitly declaring it. However, declaring variables is considered a good practice as it improves code clarity and prevents accidental overwriting of variables.

To declare a variable, use the following syntax:

variable_name=value

Here, variable_name is the name you choose for your variable, and value is the initial value you want to assign to it. It's important to note that Bash variables are untyped, meaning they can hold any type of data.

2. Assigning Values:

To assign a value to a variable, use the assignment operator (=). There should be no spaces around the assignment operator. Here's an example:

name="John"
age=25

In this case, the variable name is assigned the value "John", and the variable age is assigned the value 25.

3. Accessing Variable Values:

To access the value stored in a variable, prepend the variable name with a dollar sign ($). Here's an example:

echo $name
echo $age

These commands will output the values of the name and age variables, respectively.

4. Variable Naming Conventions:

When naming variables, it's important to follow certain conventions:

- Variable names should start with a letter or an underscore (_).
- Variable names are case-sensitive.

Avoid using special characters or spaces in variable names, as they may cause syntax errors or make your code harder to read.

5. Environment Variables:

Bash also provides a set of predefined variables called environment variables. These variables hold information about the current environment and system settings. They are typically uppercase, and some common examples include PATH, HOME, and USER.

To access the value of an environment variable, use the same syntax as accessing regular variables:

echo $PATH
echo $HOME

These commands will display the values of the PATH and HOME environment variables, respectively.

6. Readonly Variables:

You can mark variables as readonly to prevent their values from being changed. This is useful when you want to ensure that certain variables remain constant throughout the execution of your script. Here's an example:

readonly pi=3.14159

After declaring a variable as readonly, any attempt to assign a new value to it will result in an error.

Properly declaring and assigning variables in your Bash scripts is important for code clarity, readability, and maintaining script integrity. By following the conventions and best practices, you can effectively work with variables and make your scripts more robust and flexible.

5.3 Variable Scope and Lifetime

In Bash scripting, declaring and assigning variables allows you to store and manipulate data within your scripts. By properly declaring and assigning variables, you can make your scripts more readable, maintainable, and flexible. In this section, we'll explore the process of declaring and assigning variables in Bash.

1. Variable Declaration:

In Bash, variable declaration is not mandatory. You can directly assign a value to a variable without explicitly declaring it. However, declaring variables is considered a good practice as it improves code clarity and prevents accidental overwriting of variables.

To declare a variable, use the following syntax:

variable_name=value

Here, variable_name is the name you choose for your variable, and value is the initial value you want to assign to it. It's important to note that Bash variables are untyped, meaning they can hold any type of data.

2. Assigning Values:

To assign a value to a variable, use the assignment operator (=). There should be no spaces around the assignment operator. Here's an example:

name="John"
age=25

In this case, the variable name is assigned the value "John", and the variable age is assigned the value 25.

3. Accessing Variable Values:

To access the value stored in a variable, prepend the variable name with a dollar sign ($). Here's an example:

echo $name
echo $age

These commands will output the values of the name and age variables, respectively.

4. Variable Naming Conventions:

When naming variables, it's important to follow certain conventions:

Variable names should start with a letter or an underscore (_).
Variable names are case-sensitive.

Avoid using special characters or spaces in variable names, as they may cause syntax errors or make your code harder to read.

5. Environment Variables:

Bash also provides a set of predefined variables called environment variables. These variables hold information about the current environment and system settings. They are typically uppercase, and some common examples include PATH, HOME, and USER.

To access the value of an environment variable, use the same syntax as accessing regular variables:

echo $PATH
echo $HOME

These commands will display the values of the PATH and HOME environment variables, respectively.

6. Readonly Variables:

You can mark variables as readonly to prevent their values from being changed. This is useful when you want to ensure that certain variables remain constant throughout the execution of your script. Here's an example:

readonly pi=3.14159

After declaring a variable as readonly, any attempt to assign a new value to it will result in an error.

Properly declaring and assigning variables in your Bash scripts is important for code clarity, readability, and maintaining script integrity. By following the conventions and best practices, you can effectively work with variables and make your scripts more robust and flexible.

5.4 Working with Data Types: Strings, Numbers, and Arrays

In Bash scripting, you can work with different data types such as strings, numbers, and arrays. Understanding how to handle these data types is essential for performing various operations and manipulations in your scripts. In this section, we'll explore working with strings, numbers, and arrays in Bash.

1. Strings:

Strings are sequences of characters enclosed in single quotes (') or double quotes ("). Bash treats both types of quotes slightly differently, with double quotes allowing for variable expansion and command substitution.

Assigning a string to a variable:

name="John Doe"
Concatenating strings:
makefile
Copy code
greeting="Hello, "
name="John Doe"
message=$greeting$name

In this example, the message variable will contain the concatenated string "Hello, John Doe".

2. Numbers:

Bash supports arithmetic operations on numbers, although it treats all variables as strings by default. To perform numerical operations, you need to explicitly specify the variable as an integer using the declare or typeset command.

Assigning an integer to a variable:

declare -i age=25

Performing arithmetic operations:

num1=10
num2=5
sum=$((num1 + num2))

In this example, the sum variable will hold the value 15, which is the result of adding num1 and num2.

3. Arrays:

Arrays allow you to store multiple values in a single variable. In Bash, arrays are indexed starting from 0, and elements are accessed using the index value.

Declaring and assigning values to an array:

fruits=("Apple" "Banana" "Orange")

Accessing array elements:

echo ${fruits[0]}   # Output: Apple

Modifying array elements:

fruits[1]="Mango"

Looping through array elements:

for fruit in "${fruits[@]}"; do
    echo $fruit
done

This loop will iterate through all elements of the fruits array and print them one by one.

Note: Bash does not have built-in support for multi-dimensional arrays. However, you can simulate them using nested arrays.

Working with different data types in Bash allows you to manipulate and process data effectively within your scripts. By understanding the characteristics and syntax for working with strings, numbers, and arrays, you can perform a wide range of operations and create dynamic and flexible Bash scripts.

Chapter 6: Conditional Statements and Loops

In the world of scripting, conditional statements and loops are indispensable tools for controlling the flow of your code. In this chapter, we will dive into the realm of conditional statements and loops in Bash, empowering you to make decisions and automate repetitive tasks with ease.

We will begin by exploring conditional statements such as the if-else statement and the case statement. You will learn how to evaluate conditions and execute different blocks of code based on the outcome. Understanding these conditional constructs will allow you to add flexibility and logic to your scripts.

Next, we will journey into the world of loops, including the versatile for loop and the powerful while and until loops. You will discover how to iterate over collections, perform actions repeatedly, and control the loop execution based on specific conditions. Loops will become your allies in automating tasks and processing data efficiently.

By mastering conditional statements and loops, you will unlock the ability to create dynamic and intelligent scripts that adapt to different scenarios. Whether you need to make decisions based on specific conditions or repeat actions until a certain criterion is met, these constructs will be your go-to tools.

Get ready to wield the power of conditional statements and loops as we embark on this chapter. By the end, you will have the skills and knowledge to take control of your scripts, making them responsive, adaptable, and capable of handling complex tasks.

6.1 Introduction to Conditional Statements

Conditional statements in Bash scripting allow you to control the flow of your script based on certain conditions. These statements enable you to execute specific blocks of code selectively, depending on whether a condition is true or false. Conditional statements are fundamental for implementing logic and decision-making in your scripts. In this section, we'll introduce you to conditional statements in Bash.

1. The if statement:

The if statement is the most basic conditional statement in Bash. It allows you to execute a block of code only if a specific condition is true. Here's the general syntax:

if condition

then
    # code to execute if condition is true
fi

The condition can be any valid expression or command that evaluates to either true or false. If the condition is true, the code block between the then and fi keywords is executed. Otherwise, it is skipped.

Example:

age=25

if [$age -ge 18]
then
    echo "You are an adult."
fi

In this example, if the value of the age variable is greater than or equal to 18, the message "You are an adult" will be displayed.

2. The if-else statement:

The if-else statement extends the if statement by allowing you to specify an alternative code block to execute if the condition is false. Here's the syntax:

if condition
then
    # code to execute if condition is true

```
else
    # code to execute if condition is false
fi
```

If the condition is true, the code block after the then keyword is executed. Otherwise, the code block after the else keyword is executed.

Example:

```
age=15

if [ $age -ge 18 ]
then
    echo "You are an adult."
else
    echo "You are not yet an adult."
fi
```

In this example, if the value of the age variable is greater than or equal to 18, the message "You are an adult" is displayed. Otherwise, the message "You are not yet an adult" is displayed.

3. The if-elif-else statement:

The if-elif-else statement allows you to test multiple conditions sequentially. It provides a way to check for alternative conditions when the preceding conditions are false. Here's the syntax:

```
if condition1
then
    # code to execute if condition1 is true
elif condition2
then
    # code to execute if condition2 is true
else
    # code to execute if all conditions are false
fi
```

If condition1 is true, the code block after the then keyword is executed, and the rest of the if-elif-else statement is skipped. If condition1 is false, condition2 is evaluated, and if it is true, the corresponding code block is executed. If all conditions are false, the code block after the else keyword is executed.

Example:

```
score=75

if [ $score -ge 90 ]
then
    echo "Excellent!"
elif [ $score -ge 80 ]
then
    echo "Very good!"
elif [ $score -ge 70 ]
then
    echo "Good!"
else
```

```
    echo "Needs improvement."
fi
```

In this example, depending on the value of the score variable, a corresponding message is displayed.

Conditional statements provide the ability to make decisions and execute code based on certain conditions. By using if, if-else, and if-elif-else statements, you can implement different branches of logic in your Bash scripts, enabling them to respond dynamically to varying situations.

6.2 The if-else Statement

The if-else statement in Bash allows you to execute different blocks of code based on a condition. It provides an alternative code path when the condition specified in the if statement evaluates to false. The if-else statement is useful when you want to handle both true and false cases of a condition. Here's the syntax:

```
if condition
then
    # code to execute if condition is true
else
    # code to execute if condition is false
fi
```

The condition can be any valid expression or command that returns a true or false value. If the condition is true, the code block after the then keyword is executed. If the condition is false, the code block after the else keyword is executed.

Example:

age=20

```
if [ $age -ge 18 ]
then
    echo "You are an adult."
else
    echo "You are not yet an adult."
fi
```

In this example, the if statement checks if the value of the age variable is greater than or equal to 18. If it is true, the message "You are an adult" is displayed. If the condition is false, the message "You are not yet an adult" is displayed.

You can also have multiple statements within each code block. If you need to execute more than one statement, you can enclose them in a pair of curly braces {}.

Example:

age=15

```
if [ $age -ge 18 ]
then
    echo "You are eligible to vote."
    echo "Please cast your vote."
else
    echo "You are not eligible to vote."
    echo "Please wait until you turn 18."
fi
```

In this example, the code block after the then keyword contains two echo statements that will be executed if the condition is true. Similarly, the code block after the else keyword contains two echo statements that will be executed if the condition is false.

The if-else statement provides a way to handle alternative code paths based on a condition. It allows your Bash scripts to make decisions and respond accordingly. By using the if-else statement, you can create more complex logic and control the flow of your script based on different scenarios.

6.3 The case Statement

The case statement in Bash allows you to perform pattern matching against a variable or value. It provides an elegant way to handle multiple possible conditions and execute code based on the matched pattern. The case statement is particularly useful when you have a limited number of patterns to compare against. Here's the syntax:

```
case variable in
    pattern1)
        # code to execute for pattern1
        ;;
    pattern2)
        # code to execute for pattern2
        ;;
    pattern3)
        # code to execute for pattern3
        ;;
    *)
        # code to execute if no pattern matches
        ;;
esac
```

The variable is the value that you want to match against the patterns. Each pattern is followed by a set of statements to execute if the pattern matches. The ;; at the end of each code block is used to terminate the execution of that particular block.

The * symbol acts as a default pattern and matches anything that doesn't match any of the specified patterns.

Example:

fruit="apple"

```
case $fruit in
   "apple")
      echo "It's an apple."
      ;;
   "banana")
      echo "It's a banana."
      ;;
   "orange")
      echo "It's an orange."
      ;;
   *)
      echo "It's an unknown fruit."
      ;;
esac
```

In this example, the case statement checks the value of the fruit variable against different patterns. If the value is "apple", the message "It's an apple" is displayed. If it's "banana", the message "It's a banana" is displayed. If it's "orange", the message "It's an orange" is displayed. If none of the patterns match, the default message "It's an unknown fruit" is displayed.

You can also use pattern ranges and character classes in the patterns for more advanced matching. Additionally, you can have multiple patterns that execute the same code block by separating them with the | symbol.

```
case $fruit in
    "apple" | "banana" | "orange")
        echo "It's a common fruit."
        ;;
    "grape" | "kiwi" | "melon")
        echo "It's an exotic fruit."
        ;;
    *)
        echo "It's an unknown fruit."
        ;;
esac
```

In this example, if the value of $fruit matches "apple", "banana", or "orange", the message "It's a common fruit" is displayed. If it matches "grape", "kiwi", or "melon", the message "It's an exotic fruit" is displayed. If none of the patterns match, the default message "It's an unknown fruit" is displayed.

The case statement provides a flexible way to perform pattern matching and execute code based on the matched pattern. It allows you to handle multiple conditions elegantly and keep your code organized. By using the case statement, you can create versatile Bash scripts that respond to different scenarios efficiently.

6.4 Introduction to Looping

Looping is a fundamental concept in programming that allows you to repeat a set of instructions multiple times. It is an essential feature in Bash scripting to automate repetitive tasks or iterate over a collection of items. Bash provides several looping constructs to cater to different looping requirements. In this section, we will introduce you to the two main types of loops in Bash: the for loop and the while loop.

1. The for loop:

The for loop in Bash allows you to iterate over a list of items or elements. It repeatedly executes a block of code for each item in the specified list. Here's the general syntax of a for loop:

```
for variable in list
do
    # code to execute for each item
done
```

The variable represents a variable that holds each item from the list during each iteration. The list can be a sequence of values, an array, or the output of a command. The code block between do and done is executed for each item in the list.

Example:

```
fruits=("apple" "banana" "orange" "grape")
```

```
for fruit in "${fruits[@]}"
do
    echo "I like $fruit"
done
```

In this example, the for loop iterates over each item in the fruits array. During each iteration, the value of the fruit variable is set to the current item, and the message "I like <fruit>" is displayed.

2. The while loop:

The while loop in Bash repeatedly executes a block of code as long as a specified condition is true. It is useful when you want to continue looping until a certain condition is no longer satisfied. Here's the general syntax of a while loop:

```
while condition
do
    # code to execute as long as condition is true
done
```

The condition can be any valid expression or command that returns a true or false value. The code block between do and done is executed repeatedly as long as the condition remains true.

Example:

```
count=1
```

```
while [ $count -le 5 ]
do
   echo "Count: $count"
   count=$((count + 1))
done
```

In this example, the while loop executes the code block as long as the value of the count variable is less than or equal to 5. The value of count is incremented by 1 in each iteration, and the current count is displayed.

Looping allows you to automate repetitive tasks, process collections of data, and perform iterative operations in your Bash scripts. By using the for and while loops, you can efficiently handle various looping scenarios and make your scripts more dynamic and powerful.

6.5 The for Loop

The for loop is a powerful looping construct in Bash that allows you to iterate over a list of items or elements. It provides a convenient way to repeat a set of instructions for each item in the specified list. The for loop is particularly useful when you have a known number of iterations or when you want to perform a specific action for each item in a collection.

The general syntax of a for loop in Bash is as follows:

```
for variable in list
do
    # code to execute for each item
done
```

Let's break down the different components of the for loop:

variable: It represents a variable that holds each item from the list during each iteration. You can choose any valid variable name to store the current item value.

list: It can be a sequence of values, an array, or the output of a command. The for loop iterates over each item in the list, assigning the current item to the variable.

Here's an example that demonstrates the usage of a for loop:

```
fruits=("apple" "banana" "orange" "grape")

for fruit in "${fruits[@]}"
do
    echo "I like $fruit"
done
```

In this example, we have an array called fruits that contains four different fruits. The for loop iterates over each item in the fruits array. During each iteration, the value of the fruit variable is set to the current item, and the code block within the loop is executed. In this case, the code block simply echoes the message "I like <fruit>", where <fruit> is replaced with the current fruit item.

The output of this example would be:

I like apple
I like banana
I like orange
I like grape

You can also use a numerical range with the for loop to iterate over a sequence of numbers. Here's an example:

```
for number in {1..5}
do
    echo "Number: $number"
done
```

In this case, the for loop iterates over the numerical range from 1 to 5. The value of the number variable is set to each number in the range, and the code block within the loop is executed. The output would be:

Number: 1
Number: 2
Number: 3
Number: 4

Number: 5

The for loop provides a convenient way to iterate over a list of items or perform a specific action for a known number of iterations. It allows you to automate repetitive tasks, process collections of data, and handle various looping scenarios in your Bash scripts. By leveraging the power of the for loop, you can make your scripts more efficient, dynamic, and versatile.

6.6 The while and until Loops

In addition to the for loop, Bash provides two more looping constructs: the while loop and the until loop. These loops are useful when you want to repeatedly execute a block of code based on a certain condition. Unlike the for loop, which iterates over a list of items, the while and until loops execute the code block as long as a specified condition is true or false, respectively.

1. The while loop:

The while loop repeatedly executes a block of code as long as a specified condition remains true. It is commonly used when you want to continue looping until a certain condition is no longer satisfied. Here's the general syntax of a while loop:

while condition

do
    # code to execute as long as condition is true
done

The condition can be any valid expression or command that returns a true or false value. The code block between do and done is executed repeatedly as long as the condition remains true.

Here's an example that demonstrates the usage of a while loop:

count=1

while [$count -le 5]
do
   echo "Count: $count"
   count=$((count + 1))
done

In this example, the while loop executes the code block as long as the value of the count variable is less than or equal to 5. The value of count is incremented by 1 in each iteration using the (( )) arithmetic expansion syntax, and the current count is displayed. The output would be:

Count: 1
Count: 2
Count: 3
Count: 4

Count: 5

2. The until loop:

The until loop is similar to the while loop, but it repeatedly executes a block of code as long as a specified condition remains false. It is useful when you want to continue looping until a certain condition becomes true. Here's the general syntax of an until loop:

```
until condition
do
    # code to execute as long as condition is false
done
```

The condition can be any valid expression or command that returns a true or false value. The code block between do and done is executed repeatedly as long as the condition remains false.

Here's an example that demonstrates the usage of an until loop:

```
count=1

until [ $count -gt 5 ]
do
   echo "Count: $count"
   count=$((count + 1))
done
```

In this example, the until loop executes the code block as long as the value of the count variable is not greater than 5. The value of count is incremented by 1 in each iteration, and the current count is displayed. The output would be the same as the while loop example:

Count: 1
Count: 2
Count: 3
Count: 4
Count: 5

The while and until loops provide flexibility in executing a block of code based on a condition. By using these loops, you can create dynamic scripts that repeat operations until a certain condition is met or not met. Whether you need to iterate while a condition is true or until a condition becomes true, the while and until loops have you covered.

Chapter 7: Input and Output in Shell Scripts

In this chapter, we will explore the world of input and output in shell scripts. You will learn how to interact with users, read input from different sources, and display output effectively. These skills are crucial for creating interactive and user-friendly scripts.

We will delve into techniques for prompting users for input, reading input from command-line arguments, and accepting input from files. You will discover how to handle user responses and validate input to ensure your scripts operate smoothly.

Additionally, we will explore various methods of generating output, including printing messages, formatting data, and redirecting output to files. You will learn how to leverage these techniques to provide informative and organized output to users or for further processing.

By the end of this chapter, you will have a solid understanding of how to handle input and output in your shell scripts. Whether you need to create scripts that interact with users, process data from different sources, or produce well-formatted output, these skills will enable you to create robust and user-friendly scripts. Get ready to make your scripts communicate effectively with the world!

7.1 Reading User Input

In Bash scripting, you can interact with the user by reading input from the keyboard or other input sources. This allows your scripts to be more interactive and versatile. Bash provides several mechanisms for reading user input, including the read command and command-line arguments.

1. The read command:

The read command is used to prompt the user for input and store the entered value in a variable. It waits for the user to input a line of text and press Enter. The general syntax of the read command is as follows:

read variable_name

After executing the read command, the user's input is assigned to the specified variable_name. You can then use the variable to access and process the user's input in your script.

Here's an example that demonstrates the usage of the read command:

```
echo "What is your name?"
read name
echo "Hello, $name! Nice to meet you."
```

In this example, the script prompts the user to enter their name using the read command. The entered name is stored in the name variable. The script then displays a greeting message using the entered name.

2. Command-line arguments:

Another way to read user input is by using command-line arguments. Command-line arguments are values passed to a script when it is executed. You can access these arguments inside your script using special variables: $1, $2, $3, and so on. Here, $1 represents the first argument, $2 represents the second argument, and so on.

Here's an example that demonstrates the usage of command-line arguments:

script name: greeting.sh

echo "Hello, $1! Nice to meet you."

If you run the script with the command bash greeting.sh John, the output would be:

Hello, John! Nice to meet you.

In this example, the script expects the user to provide a name as the first command-line argument. The script then accesses the argument using $1 and incorporates it into the greeting message.

Command-line arguments provide a convenient way to pass input to your script when invoking it, allowing for more flexibility and automation.

By utilizing the read command and command-line arguments, you can incorporate user input into your Bash scripts, making them more interactive and adaptable to various scenarios. Whether you need to prompt the user for specific information or process command-line arguments, these techniques enable you to create dynamic and user-friendly scripts.

7.2 Displaying Output to the User

In Bash scripting, displaying output to the user is essential for providing information, progress updates, or results. Bash provides various mechanisms for outputting text and data to the user, including the echo command, command substitution, and formatted output using printf.

1. The echo command:

The echo command is the simplest way to display text or variables on the screen. It takes one or more arguments and prints them to the standard output.

The general syntax of the echo command is as follows:

echo argument1 argument2 ..
.

Here's an example that demonstrates the usage of the echo command:

echo "Hello, World!"

In this example, the script uses the echo command to display the text "Hello, World!" on the screen.

You can also use variables with the echo command to display their values. For example:

name="John"
echo "Hello, $name!"

In this case, the echo command outputs the message "Hello, John!" by incorporating the value of the name variable.

2. Command substitution:

Command substitution allows you to capture the output of a command and use it as part of another command or in a variable assignment. It is denoted by $(command) or the older backtick syntax `command`.

The command within the substitution is executed, and its output is substituted in place.

Here's an example that demonstrates the usage of command substitution:

files_count=$(ls | wc -l)
echo "The current directory contains $files_count files."

In this example, the ls | wc -l command is executed within the command substitution. It lists the files in the current directory and counts the number of lines (which corresponds to the number of files). The output of the command is captured and assigned to the files_count variable. The script then displays the number of files in the current directory.

3. Formatted output with printf:

The printf command allows you to format and display output in a more precise and controlled manner. It provides a way to specify placeholders and format specifiers to represent values dynamically. The general syntax of the printf command is as follows:

printf format_string [arguments...]

Here's an example that demonstrates the usage of printf:

```
name="Alice"
age=25
printf "Name: %s\nAge: %d\n" "$name" "$age"
```

In this example, the printf command uses format specifiers %s and %d to represent the name and age values, respectively. The values are provided as additional arguments after the format string.

The output of the printf command would be:

```
Name: Alice
Age: 25
```

By utilizing the echo command, command substitution, and printf, you can effectively display output to the user in your Bash scripts. Whether you need to show simple text, incorporate variables, or format the output, these techniques provide you with the necessary tools to convey information effectively.

7.3 Working with Files and Directories

In Bash scripting, you often need to interact with files and directories, performing operations such as creating, modifying, or deleting them. Bash provides a variety of commands and operators to handle file and directory operations efficiently.

1. File Operations:

Creating a file: The touch command is used to create an empty file or update the timestamp of an existing file. For example, touch myfile.txt creates a new file named myfile.txt if it doesn't exist.

Copying a file: The cp command is used to copy files. For example, cp file1.txt file2.txt creates a copy of file1.txt named file2.txt.

Moving or renaming a file: The mv command is used to move or rename files. For example, mv oldname.txt newname.txt renames oldname.txt to newname.txt.

Deleting a file: The rm command is used to remove/delete files. For example, rm myfile.txt deletes the file myfile.txt.

2. Directory Operations:

Creating a directory: The mkdir command is used to create a new directory. For example, mkdir mydir creates a new directory named mydir.

Copying a directory: The cp command with the -r option is used to copy directories recursively. For example, cp -r dir1 dir2 copies dir1 and its contents to dir2.

Moving or renaming a directory: The mv command is used to move or rename directories. For example, mv olddir newdir renames olddir to newdir.

Deleting a directory: The rm command with the -r option is used to remove/delete directories and their contents recursively. For example, rm -r mydir deletes the directory mydir and its contents.

3. File and Directory Permissions:

Changing permissions: The chmod command is used to change the permissions of files and directories. For example, chmod +x script.sh adds executable permission to the file script.sh.

Viewing permissions: The ls command with the -l option displays the permissions of files and directories. For example, ls -l myfile.txt shows the permissions of myfile.txt along with other details.

4. File and Directory Information:

Listing files and directories: The ls command is used to list files and directories in a directory. For example, ls lists the files and directories in the current directory.

Displaying file content: The cat command is used to display the contents of a file. For example, cat myfile.txt shows the contents of myfile.txt on the terminal.

Finding files: The find command is used to search for files and directories based on various criteria. For example, find /path/to/search -name "*.txt" finds all files with the .txt extension in the specified path.

These are just a few examples of the many file and directory operations you can perform in Bash scripting. By using the appropriate commands and operators, you can manipulate files and directories to meet your script's requirements.

Chapter 8: String Manipulation and Text Processing

Strings are a fundamental component of shell scripting, and in this chapter, we will explore the art of string manipulation and text processing in Bash. You will discover powerful techniques to manipulate and transform strings, allowing you to extract valuable information and modify data within your scripts.

We will delve into a variety of string operations, including concatenation, substring extraction, searching, and replacing. You will learn how to manipulate strings using parameter expansion, command substitution, and built-in string manipulation functions, enabling you to perform complex transformations with ease.

Furthermore, we will dive into the world of text processing, where you will discover techniques for manipulating and analyzing text data. You will learn how to use pattern matching with regular expressions, apply filtering and transformation operations with tools like awk and sed, and process structured data with tools like cut and tr.

By mastering string manipulation and text processing, you will unlock the ability to extract valuable insights from textual data, automate text-related tasks, and streamline your scripting workflow. Get ready to harness the power of strings and dive into the fascinating world of text processing in Bash!

8.1 String Concatenation and Manipulation

In Bash scripting, string manipulation is a common task that involves combining strings, extracting substrings, replacing text, and performing various operations on strings. Bash provides several techniques and built-in functions to manipulate and concatenate strings effectively.

1. String Concatenation:

To concatenate strings in Bash, you can simply use the concatenation operator + or by enclosing the strings within double quotes. Here are some examples:

```
str1="Hello"
str2="World"
concatenated_str=$str1$str2
echo $concatenated_str   # Output: HelloWorld

concatenated_str="$str1 $str2"
echo $concatenated_str   # Output: Hello World
```

In the first example, the strings str1 and str2 are concatenated without any space. In the second example, the strings are concatenated with a space in between.

2. Substring Extraction:

To extract a substring from a larger string, you can use the ${string:start_index:length} syntax. Here's an example:

str="Hello World"
substring=${str:0:5}
echo $substring   # Output: Hello

In this example, the substring is extracted from the str variable, starting from index 0 and having a length of 5 characters.

3. String Length:

To determine the length of a string, you can use the ${#string} syntax. Here's an example:

str="Hello"
length=${#str}
echo $length   # Output: 5

In this example, the length of the str variable is computed and stored in the length variable.

4. String Replacement:

Bash provides various methods to replace substrings within a string. Here are a few examples:

Using the ${string/substring/replacement} syntax:

bash
Copy code
```
str="Hello World"
replaced_str=${str/World/Universe}
echo $replaced_str   # Output: Hello Universe
```

Using the ${string//substring/replacement} syntax to replace all occurrences:

```
str="Hello World World"
replaced_str=${str//World/Universe}
echo $replaced_str     # Output: Hello Universe Universe
```

5. String Manipulation Functions:

Bash provides various built-in functions for string manipulation. Here are a few commonly used ones:

toupper and tolower functions to convert the string to uppercase or lowercase, respectively:

str="Hello"

```
uppercase_str=${str^^}
echo $uppercase_str   # Output: HELLO

lowercase_str=${str,,}
echo $lowercase_str   # Output: hello
```

trim function to remove leading and trailing whitespace:

bash
Copy code
```
str="  Hello World  "
trimmed_str=${str##*( )}
trimmed_str=${trimmed_str%%*( )}
echo $trimmed_str   # Output: Hello World
```

These are just a few examples of string manipulation in Bash scripting. Bash provides many more features and functions to work with strings efficiently. By leveraging these techniques, you can manipulate and modify strings as needed in your scripts.

8.2 Pattern Matching and Substring Extraction

Pattern matching and substring extraction are powerful techniques in Bash scripting that allow you to search for specific patterns within strings and extract relevant substrings. Bash provides various operators and constructs for pattern matching and substring extraction, such as glob patterns, regular expressions, and string manipulation functions.

1. Glob Patterns:

Glob patterns are a simple and commonly used form of pattern matching in Bash. They allow you to match filenames or strings based on wildcard characters. Here are some examples:

- *: Matches any sequence of characters.
- ?: Matches any single character.
- [characters]: Matches any character within the specified set.
- [!characters]: Matches any character not within the specified set.

Here's an example that demonstrates the usage of glob patterns:

```
files=(file1.txt file2.txt image.jpg script.sh)
for file in "${files[@]}"; do
  if [[ $file == *.txt ]]; then
    echo "Text file: $file"
  fi
done
```

In this example, the script uses the *.txt glob pattern to match all files with the .txt extension and prints their names.

2. Regular Expressions:

Regular expressions (regex) provide a more advanced and flexible form of pattern matching in Bash. They allow you to define complex patterns and perform sophisticated matching and extraction operations. Bash provides the =~ operator to apply regular expressions to strings.

Here's an example that demonstrates the usage of regular expressions:

```
str="Hello, 123 World!"
if [[ $str =~ [0-9]+ ]]; then
  echo "Number found: ${BASH_REMATCH[0]}"
fi
```

In this example, the script uses the regular expression [0-9]+ to match one or more digits within the string. If a match is found, the script outputs the matched number using the ${BASH_REMATCH[0]} variable.

3. String Manipulation Functions:

Bash provides various built-in functions that can be used to manipulate strings and extract substrings based on specific patterns. Here are a few examples:

- ${string#substring}: Removes the shortest match of substring from the beginning of string.

- ${string##substring}: Removes the longest match of substring from the beginning of string.
- ${string%substring}: Removes the shortest match of substring from the end of string.
- ${string%%substring}: Removes the longest match of substring from the end of string.
- ${string/pattern/replacement}: Replaces the first occurrence of pattern with replacement in string.
- ${string//pattern/replacement}: Replaces all occurrences of pattern with replacement in string.

Here's an example that demonstrates the usage of string manipulation functions:

```
str="Hello, World!"
echo ${str#Hello, }    # Output: World!
echo ${str%!*}         # Output: Hello, World
echo ${str/World/Universe} # Output: Hello, Universe!
```

In this example, various string manipulation functions are used to remove substrings from the beginning and end of str, as well as replace specific patterns within the string.

Pattern matching and substring extraction provide powerful capabilities for searching, matching, and extracting relevant information from strings in Bash scripting. By leveraging glob patterns, regular expressions, and string manipulation functions, you can handle complex pattern matching tasks efficiently in your scripts.

8.3 Text Manipulation with Regular Expressions

Regular expressions (regex) are a powerful tool for text manipulation in Bash scripting. They allow you to define complex patterns and perform advanced search and replacement operations within text data. Bash provides several tools and operators for working with regular expressions, enabling you to manipulate and transform text efficiently.

1. Pattern Matching with Regular Expressions:

Bash provides the =~ operator to match a string against a regular expression. Here's an example:

```
str="Hello, World!"
if [[ $str =~ ^Hello ]]; then
  echo "String starts with 'Hello'"
fi
```

In this example, the script checks if the str variable starts with the word "Hello" using the ^ symbol to anchor the pattern to the beginning of the string.

2. Extraction with Regular Expressions:

Regular expressions can be used to extract specific portions of text from a larger string. Bash provides the ${BASH_REMATCH[n]} array variable to store the matched substrings. Here's an example:

```
str="Hello, World!"
if [[ $str =~ ([A-Za-z]+), ([A-Za-z]+) ]]; then
  echo "First word: ${BASH_REMATCH[1]}"
  echo "Second word: ${BASH_REMATCH[2]}"
fi
```

In this example, the script extracts the first and second words from the str variable, assuming they consist of alphabetical characters. The captured substrings are stored in ${BASH_REMATCH[1]} and ${BASH_REMATCH[2]} respectively.

3. Text Replacement with Regular Expressions:

Bash provides the ${string//pattern/replacement} syntax to perform global text replacement using regular expressions. Here's an example:

```
str="Hello, World!"
replaced_str=${str//Hello/Hi}
echo $replaced_str   # Output: Hi, World!
```

In this example, the script replaces all occurrences of "Hello" with "Hi" using the ${string//pattern/replacement} syntax.

4. Sed - Stream Editor:

The sed command is a powerful tool for text manipulation that supports regular expressions. It allows you to perform various operations such as substitution, deletion, insertion, and more on lines of text. Here's an example:

```
str="Hello, World!"
replaced_str=$(echo $str | sed 's/Hello/Hi/')
echo $replaced_str   # Output: Hi, World!
```

In this example, the sed command is used with the s/Hello/Hi/ expression to replace the first occurrence of "Hello" with "Hi" in the input string.

Regular expressions provide extensive capabilities for text manipulation in Bash scripting. By mastering regular expressions and utilizing tools like =~ operator and sed command, you can perform advanced search, extraction, and replacement operations on text data to meet your script's requirements.

8.4 Using awk and sed for Text Processing

In Bash scripting, the awk and sed commands are powerful tools for text processing and manipulation. They allow you to perform various operations on text data, such as searching, filtering, replacing, and extracting specific fields. Understanding how to utilize awk and sed can greatly enhance your ability to process and transform text efficiently.

1. awk Command:

The awk command is a versatile tool for processing structured text data. It operates on records (lines) and fields within those records. Here are some common use cases:

Printing specific fields:

echo "John Doe,30" | awk -F',' '{print $1}'   # Output: John Doe

In this example, the -F',' option sets the field separator as a comma, and $1 refers to the first field. The command prints the first field from the input.

Applying conditions and filters:

```
cat data.txt | awk '$3 > 50 {print $1, $3}'   # Output: John 60
```

This example reads data from data.txt and prints the first and third fields if the third field is greater than 50.

Performing calculations:

```
cat grades.txt | awk '{total += $2; count++} END {print "Average:", total/count}'
```

In this example, the command calculates the average of the second field (grades) from the grades.txt file.

2. sed Command:

The sed command (stream editor) is primarily used for text transformations and substitutions. It operates on a line-by-line basis and applies rules to modify the input text. Here are some common use cases:

Replacing text:

```
echo "Hello, World!" | sed 's/Hello/Hi/'   # Output: Hi, World!
```

This example replaces the word "Hello" with "Hi" in the input string.

Deleting lines:

sed '/^$/d' file.txt

This command deletes empty lines from file.txt.

Extracting specific lines:

sed -n '5,10p' file.txt

This command prints lines 5 to 10 from file.txt.

3. Combining awk and sed:

awk and sed can be combined to perform complex text processing tasks. For example:

cat data.txt | sed '/Pattern/d' | awk '{print $1}' | sed 's/old/new/g'

In this example, sed is used to delete lines matching a specific pattern, then awk extracts the first field, and finally sed performs a global replacement of a specific string.

Understanding and utilizing awk and sed effectively can significantly streamline your text processing tasks. By leveraging their powerful features and combining them with other command-line tools, you can manipulate, transform, and extract valuable information from text data efficiently in your Bash scripts.

Chapter 9: File and Directory Operations

In this chapter, we will explore the realm of file and directory operations in Bash scripting. Files and directories are essential components of any system, and understanding how to interact with them programmatically is crucial for automating tasks and managing data effectively.

We will start by covering basic file operations such as creating, reading, writing, and deleting files. You will learn how to navigate directories, list their contents, and manipulate file permissions and ownership.

Furthermore, we will delve into advanced file and directory operations, including searching for files, copying and moving files, and working with file attributes and metadata. You will gain the skills to automate file management tasks and process large amounts of data efficiently.

Additionally, we will explore directory operations, such as creating and removing directories, traversing directory structures recursively, and working with symbolic links. You will discover techniques to navigate and manipulate directories with ease.

By the end of this chapter, you will have a solid understanding of file and directory operations in Bash.

Whether you need to organize and manipulate files, search for specific data, or automate file management tasks, this knowledge will empower you to create powerful and efficient scripts. Get ready to navigate the file system and master the art of file and directory operations!

9.1 Working with Files: Creating, Reading, and Writing

In Bash scripting, working with files is a common task. Whether you need to create new files, read data from existing files, or write data to files, understanding file manipulation is essential. This chapter covers the basics of file handling in Bash, including creating, reading, and writing files.

1. Creating Files:

To create a new file in Bash, you can use the touch command. Here's an example:

touch myfile.txt

This command creates a new file named myfile.txt in the current directory. If the file already exists, touch updates its modification timestamp.

2. Reading Files:

Bash provides various tools to read data from files. One common tool is the cat command, which displays the contents of a file. Here's an example:

```
cat myfile.txt
```

This command reads and displays the contents of myfile.txt on the terminal.

Another useful tool is the read command, which allows you to read data from a file line by line within a script. Here's an example:

```
while IFS= read -r line; do
  echo "Line: $line"
done < myfile.txt
```

In this example, the script reads each line from myfile.txt and prints it with the prefix "Line: ".

3. Writing to Files:

To write data to a file, you can use the output redirection operator (> or >>). The > operator overwrites the file with new content, while the >> operator appends data to the existing file. Here are examples of both:

```
echo "Hello, World!" > myfile.txt    # Overwrite the file with new content
```

echo "Welcome!" >> myfile.txt   # Append data to the file

In the first example, the echo command writes "Hello, World!" to myfile.txt, replacing its previous content. In the second example, "Welcome!" is appended to the end of the file.

4. Removing Files:

To remove a file, you can use the rm command. Here's an example:

rm myfile.txt

This command deletes the file myfile.txt from the file system.

5. File Permissions:

Bash provides the chmod command to modify file permissions. Here's an example:

chmod +x script.sh

This command adds the executable permission to the file script.sh, allowing it to be executed as a script.

Understanding how to create, read, write, and delete files in Bash is essential for file manipulation tasks. By leveraging tools like touch, cat, read, and output redirection operators, you can efficiently handle file operations within your Bash scripts. Additionally, being familiar with file permissions using chmod ensures proper control over file access and execution.

9.2 File Permissions and Ownership

In Bash scripting, understanding and managing file permissions and ownership is crucial for maintaining the security and integrity of your files. This chapter explores the concepts of file permissions and ownership in Linux, along with the commands and techniques used to modify them.

1. File Permissions:

Linux file permissions determine the access rights for users (owners), groups, and others. Permissions are represented by three sets of characters: read (r), write (w), and execute (x). Here's an example of file permissions:

-rw-r--r-- 1 user group 1234 Jun 1 10:00 myfile.txt

In this example, the first character (-) represents the file type (in this case, a regular file). The next three characters (rw-) indicate the owner's permissions (read and write), followed by three characters (r--) for the group's permissions, and another three characters (r--) for others' permissions.

To modify file permissions, you can use the chmod command. Here are some common examples:

- chmod u+x script.sh   # Adds execute permission for the owner
- chmod g-w myfile.txt   # Removes write permission for the group
- chmod o+r myfile.txt   # Adds read permission for others
- chmod 754 script.sh   # Sets permissions as rw-r-xr–

2. File Ownership:

In Linux, each file is associated with an owner and a group. The owner has specific permissions on the file, and the group consists of multiple users who share certain permissions. To view and modify file ownership, you can use the chown and chgrp commands.

- chown user myfile.txt   # Changes the owner of the file to "user"
- chgrp group myfile.txt   # Changes the group of the file to "group"

3. Special Permissions:

Linux also provides special permissions for files:

132

- Setuid (s): Executes the file with the privileges of the owner.
- Setgid (s): Executes the file with the privileges of the group.
- Sticky bit (t): Restricts file deletion by users other than the owner.

To set these special permissions, you can use the numeric mode or symbolic mode with chmod.

4. Viewing File Permissions and Ownership:

To view file permissions and ownership, you can use the ls command with the -l option:

ls -l myfile.txt

This command displays detailed information about the file, including permissions, ownership, size, modification time, and more.

Understanding and properly managing file permissions and ownership is essential for maintaining security and controlling access to your files. By utilizing commands such as chmod, chown, and chgrp, you can effectively set permissions and ownership according to your requirements. Regularly reviewing and adjusting file permissions is a good practice to ensure the security and integrity of your Bash scripts and associated files.

9.3 File and Directory Navigation

In Bash scripting, being able to navigate through the file system is essential for locating, accessing, and manipulating files and directories. This chapter covers the basic commands and techniques for file and directory navigation in the Bash shell.

1. Current Working Directory:

The current working directory refers to the directory you are currently operating in. To determine the current working directory, you can use the pwd command:

pwd

This command displays the absolute path of the current working directory.

2. Listing Files and Directories:

To list the files and directories within a directory, you can use the ls command:

ls

By default, ls lists the files and directories in the current directory. You can also provide a specific directory path as an argument to list its contents.

3. Changing Directories:

To change the current working directory, you can use the cd command:

cd /path/to/directory

This command changes the current working directory to the specified directory path. You can use both absolute and relative paths with cd.

Here are some examples of using cd:

- cd /home/user/Documents   # Change to an absolute path
- cd ../folder   # Change to a relative path (one level up)
- cd ~   # Change to the home directory
- cd -   # Change to the previous directory

4. Creating Directories:

To create a new directory, you can use the mkdir command:

mkdir new_directory

This command creates a new directory named new_directory in the current working directory. You can provide an absolute or relative path to create directories in different locations.

5. Removing Files and Directories:

To remove a file, you can use the rm command:

rm myfile.txt

This command deletes the file named myfile.txt. Be cautious when using rm as it permanently deletes files without confirmation.

To remove an empty directory, you can use the rmdir command:

rmdir empty_directory

If the directory contains files or other directories, you can use the rm command with the -r option to recursively remove the directory and its contents.

6. Moving and Renaming Files and Directories:

To move or rename a file or directory, you can use the mv command:

- mv file.txt /path/to/new_location/file.txt   # Move the file to a new location
- mv old_directory new_directory   # Rename the directory

The mv command can be used to move files and directories to different locations or rename them within the same location.

Navigating the file system effectively is essential for managing files and directories in Bash scripting. By utilizing commands like cd, ls, mkdir, rm, and mv, you can easily navigate through directories, list their contents, create and remove files and directories, and perform file and directory operations efficiently.

9.4 File and Directory Manipulation

In Bash scripting, manipulating files and directories is a common task that involves operations such as copying, moving, renaming, and searching. This chapter explores various commands and techniques for performing file and directory manipulation tasks in the Bash shell.

1. Copying Files and Directories:

To copy files and directories, you can use the cp command:

- cp file.txt /path/to/destination/   # Copy a file to a new location
- cp -r directory /path/to/destination/ # Copy a directory and its contents

The -r option is used to recursively copy directories and their contents. It's essential to specify the correct source and destination paths to ensure accurate copying.

2. Moving and Renaming Files and Directories:

To move or rename files and directories, you can use the mv command:

- mv file.txt /path/to/destination/   # Move a file to a new location
- mv directory /path/to/destination/   # Move a directory to a new location
- mv old_name new_name   # Rename a file or directory

The mv command allows you to move files and directories to different locations or rename them within the same location. Ensure that the destination path is correctly specified.

3. Removing Files and Directories:

To remove files and directories, you can use the rm command:

rm file.txt   # Remove a file

```
rm -r directory          # Remove a directory and its contents
```

The -r option is used to recursively remove directories and their contents. Be cautious when using rm as it permanently deletes files and directories without confirmation.

4. Finding Files and Directories:

To search for files and directories within a specified location, you can use the find command:

```
find /path/to/search -name "*.txt"     # Find all text files within a directory
```

The -name option is used to specify a search pattern. In the example above, the pattern "*.txt" matches all files with the ".txt" extension.

5. File Compression and Archiving:

Bash provides commands for compressing and archiving files:

- gzip and gunzip: Compress and decompress files with the gzip algorithm.
- tar: Create an archive (tarball) of files and directories.

- gzip file.txt   # Compress a file using gzip
- gunzip file.txt.gz   # Decompress a gzip-compressed file
- tar -czvf archive.tar.gz file1.txt file2.txt   # Create a compressed tarball
- tar -xzvf archive.tar.gz   # Extract files from a tarball

These commands allow you to compress individual files or create compressed archives of multiple files and directories.

File and directory manipulation is a fundamental aspect of Bash scripting. By utilizing commands like cp, mv, rm, find, and file compression utilities like gzip and tar, you can efficiently perform operations such as copying, moving, renaming, searching, and archiving files and directories.

Chapter 10: Functions and Modular Programming

Functions are the building blocks of modular and reusable code in Bash scripting. In this chapter, we will dive into the world of functions and explore how they can enhance the structure, readability, and reusability of your scripts.

We will begin by understanding the fundamentals of functions, including function declaration, parameter passing, and return values. You will learn how to create functions to encapsulate specific tasks and how to invoke them within your scripts.

Next, we will explore the concept of modular programming, where you will learn how to break down your scripts into smaller, manageable functions. You will discover the benefits of modular programming, including code organization, code reuse, and easier maintenance.

Additionally, we will cover advanced topics such as local and global variables within functions, variable scope, and function recursion. You will gain a deeper understanding of how functions interact with the overall script and how to handle variables in a modular context.

By the end of this chapter, you will have a solid understanding of functions and modular programming in Bash. You will be able to create well-structured scripts with reusable code blocks, enhancing your productivity and promoting code maintainability. Get ready to unlock the power of functions and elevate your scripting skills to a new level of modularity!

10.1 Introduction to Functions

Functions are a crucial aspect of Bash scripting as they allow you to encapsulate reusable blocks of code. This chapter introduces the concept of functions in Bash and explores their syntax, usage, and benefits.

1. What is a Function?

A function is a named block of code that performs a specific task. It helps in modularizing your script by dividing it into logical sections. Functions can be called multiple times within a script, allowing for code reuse and improved maintainability.

2. Syntax of Function Declaration:

The syntax for declaring a function in Bash is as follows:

function_name() {

    # Function body
    # Code statements
}

The function_name is the unique identifier for the function. The function body consists of the code statements enclosed within the curly braces {}.

3. Function Parameters:

Functions can accept parameters, allowing you to pass values to them. The parameters are referenced using special variables called positional parameters: $1, $2, $3, and so on. The value of $1 refers to the first parameter, $2 to the second parameter, and so on.

Here's an example of a function with parameters:

```
greet() {
    echo "Hello, $1!"
}
```

Calling the function with a parameter
greet "John"

In this example, the function greet accepts one parameter. When the function is called with the argument "John", it echoes the greeting "Hello, John!".

4. Returning Values from Functions:

Functions in Bash can also return values using the return statement. The returned value can be captured and used in the calling part of the script.

Here's an example of a function that returns a value:

```
add() {
   local sum=$(( $1 + $2 ))
   return $sum
}
```

```
# Calling the function and capturing the return value
result=$(add 10 5)
echo "The sum is: $result"
```

In this example, the add function takes two parameters and calculates their sum. The sum is stored in the sum variable and returned using the return statement. The returned value is then captured in the result variable and printed.

5. Benefits of Using Functions:

Using functions in Bash scripting offers several benefits:

- **Code Reusability**: Functions allow you to write modular code that can be reused in multiple parts of your script.

- **Modularity**: Functions help in organizing and structuring your code, making it more manageable and maintainable.
- **Encapsulation**: Functions encapsulate specific tasks, making the code more readable and easier to understand.
- **Parameterization**: Functions can accept parameters, making them adaptable to different scenarios.
- **Code Debugging**: Functions isolate specific blocks of code, making it easier to debug and fix issues.

Understanding functions and their usage in Bash scripting is essential for writing efficient and modular scripts. By encapsulating code blocks, accepting parameters, and returning values, functions enable you to create reusable and maintainable code.

10.2 Creating and Invoking Functions

Creating and invoking functions are fundamental operations in Bash scripting. This section explores the process of creating functions, defining their behavior, and invoking them within a script.

1. Function Creation:

To create a function in Bash, you need to define its name and the code block that comprises its body. The basic syntax for creating a function is as follows:

```
function_name() {
   # Function body
   # Code statements
}
```

The function_name is the unique identifier for the function, and the function body contains the code statements enclosed within the curly braces {}.

2. Invoking a Function:

To invoke or call a function, you simply need to reference its name followed by parentheses. Here's an example:

```
my_function    # Calling the function
```

When a function is called, the code inside its body is executed, and any instructions within the function are executed in order.

3. Function Parameters:

Functions in Bash can accept parameters, allowing you to pass values to them. The parameters are referenced using special variables called positional parameters: $1, $2, $3, and so on. The value of $1 refers to the first parameter, $2 to the second parameter, and so on.

Here's an example of a function with parameters:

```
greet() {
   echo "Hello, $1!"
}
```

greet "John"   # Calling the function with a parameter

In this example, the greet function accepts one parameter. When the function is called with the argument "John", it echoes the greeting "Hello, John!".

4. Returning Values:

Functions in Bash can also return values using the return statement. The returned value can be captured and used in the calling part of the script.

Here's an example of a function that returns a value:

bash
Copy code
```
add() {
   local sum=$(( $1 + $2 ))
   return $sum
}
```

```
result=$(add 10 5)    # Calling the function and
capturing the return value
echo "The sum is: $result"
```

In this example, the add function takes two parameters and calculates their sum. The sum is stored in the sum variable and returned using the return statement. The returned value is then captured in the result variable and printed.

5. Best Practices:

When creating and invoking functions, it's important to follow some best practices:

- Define functions before calling them to ensure they are available when needed.
- Give meaningful names to functions that reflect their purpose and functionality.
- Use comments within the function body to provide clarity and enhance understanding.
- Avoid using global variables within functions to maintain encapsulation.
- Provide appropriate error handling and validation within functions to handle unexpected scenarios.

Creating and invoking functions in Bash scripting allows you to encapsulate code, improve code organization, and promote code reuse. By utilizing function parameters and return values, you can create versatile and modular scripts that perform specific tasks efficiently.

10.3 Function Parameters and Return Values

Function parameters and return values play a vital role in Bash scripting as they enable flexibility and data interchangeability within functions. This section explores the usage of function parameters to pass values into functions and the return values to retrieve results from functions.

1. Function Parameters:

Function parameters allow you to pass values to functions, making them more adaptable and versatile. Parameters are referenced using positional parameters: $1, $2, $3, and so on, where $1 represents the first parameter, $2 represents the second, and so on.

Here's an example of a function with parameters:

```
greet() {
   echo "Hello, $1! Welcome to $2!"
}
```

greet "John" "Bash Scripting"   # Calling the function with two parameters

In this example, the greet function accepts two parameters. When the function is called with arguments "John" and "Bash Scripting", it echoes the greeting "Hello, John! Welcome to Bash Scripting!".

You can access and use these parameters within the function body to perform specific operations or calculations.

2. Return Values:

Return values allow functions to provide results or data back to the calling part of the script. In Bash, you can use the return statement to specify the value to be returned.

Here's an example of a function that returns a value:

```
add() {
   local sum=$(( $1 + $2 ))
   return $sum
}

result=$(add 10 5)    # Calling the function and capturing the return value
echo "The sum is: $result"
```

In this example, the add function takes two parameters and calculates their sum. The sum is stored in the sum variable and returned using the return statement. The returned value is then captured in the result variable and printed.

You can use the returned value in subsequent operations or assign it to a variable for further processing.

3. Passing Arrays as Parameters:

In addition to individual values, Bash functions can also accept arrays as parameters. You can pass an entire array or specific elements of an array to a function.

```
process_array() {
    local array=("$@")   # Retrieve all parameters as an array
    # Process the array elements
}

my_array=("apple" "banana" "orange")
process_array "${my_array[@]}"      # Passing the entire array as a parameter
```

In this example, the process_array function accepts an array as a parameter using the "$@" syntax. The entire array my_array is passed to the function using "${my_array[@]}".

4. Multiple Return Values:

Bash does not provide native support for multiple return values from a function. However, you can use various techniques to achieve a similar result, such as using arrays or global variables to store and retrieve multiple values.

```
get_values() {
   local value1="Hello"
   local value2="World"
    # Store the values in global variables or return as an array
}

# Call the function and retrieve multiple values
get_values
echo "Value 1: $value1"
echo "Value 2: $value2"
```

In this example, the get_values function assigns values to value1 and value2 variables. These variables can be accessed outside the function since they are defined as global variables.

Using arrays or global variables allows you to emulate multiple return values from functions.

Understanding function parameters and return values is crucial for building versatile and reusable Bash scripts. By passing values through parameters and capturing return values, you can create functions that interact with the script's data and provide valuable results for further processing.

10.4 Organizing Code into Modules

As Bash scripts grow in complexity, it becomes essential to organize the code into modular components for better maintainability and reusability. Modules allow you to encapsulate related functions and variables, providing a structured approach to script development. This section explores techniques for organizing Bash code into modules.

1. Modularizing Bash Code:

Modularizing code involves breaking down the script into logical units, where each unit serves a specific purpose or handles a particular task. These units are typically implemented as separate files, often referred to as modules or libraries. Each module focuses on a specific aspect of the script's functionality and contains related functions, variables, and possibly configuration settings.

2. Creating Module Files:

To create a module file, you can either create a separate Bash script containing the functions and variables related to a particular module or define a set of functions within a script file. The latter approach is commonly used when dealing with smaller projects.

For example, you can create a module file named file_operations.sh that contains functions related to file operations, such as creating, reading, and writing files. Another module file named string_operations.sh can contain functions specifically for string manipulation and processing.

3. Importing Modules:

To use the functions and variables defined in a module, you need to import or include the module into your main script. This is achieved by sourcing the module file using the source command or the . (dot) operator followed by the path to the module file.

source file_operations.sh   # Sourcing the module file

. string_operations.sh   # Alternative syntax to source the module file

By sourcing the module files, you make their functions and variables available within the main script. This allows you to use the module's functionality seamlessly.

4. Organizing Function Names:

When creating modules, it's a good practice to prefix or namespace function names to avoid naming conflicts with other modules or functions. This helps maintain clarity and avoids unintended function name collisions. For example, if you have a module named file_operations.sh, you can prefix the functions within that module with file_ to create distinct names like file_read, file_write, etc.

5. Code Reusability and Encapsulation:

Modularizing code promotes code reusability, as you can easily import and use the same module in multiple scripts. It also enhances encapsulation, as each module operates independently, making it easier to maintain and update specific functionality without affecting the entire script.

6. Managing Module Dependencies:

In some cases, modules may have dependencies on other modules or external utilities. It's important to manage these dependencies properly. Ensure that the required modules are sourced before using functions from dependent modules. Additionally, handle any missing dependencies gracefully by providing appropriate error messages or handling mechanisms.

7. Documentation and Naming Conventions:

When creating modules, it's crucial to document their purpose, functionality, and usage. This documentation can be included within the module file itself or in a separate documentation file. Additionally, follow consistent naming conventions for module files and functions to maintain clarity and ease of understanding.

8. Testing and Maintenance:

Modular code lends itself well to testing and maintenance. You can create separate test scripts that focus on individual modules, allowing you to validate their functionality independently. This makes it easier to identify and fix issues within specific modules, ensuring the overall integrity of the script.

Organizing code into modules is a powerful technique for managing complexity and improving the maintainability of Bash scripts. By encapsulating related functions and variables into modules, you can create reusable components, promote code reuse, and enhance the overall structure and readability of your scripts.

Chapter 11: Error Handling and Debugging

In this chapter, we will explore the vital aspects of error handling and debugging in Bash scripting. No script is flawless, and understanding how to effectively handle errors and debug your code is essential for producing robust and reliable scripts.

We will start by discussing error handling techniques, including handling command failures, detecting and handling errors within scripts, and gracefully handling unexpected situations. You will learn how to implement error reporting mechanisms, handle errors with conditional statements, and incorporate error codes and error messages into your scripts.

Next, we will delve into the world of debugging. You will discover techniques for identifying and resolving issues within your scripts, including using debugging flags, tracing commands, and utilizing tools like echo and set -x. We will also explore techniques for logging and analyzing script execution to track down bugs effectively.

Moreover, we will cover best practices for error handling and debugging, including writing informative error messages, logging errors, and utilizing defensive programming techniques. You will learn how to anticipate and handle errors proactively, leading to more robust and resilient scripts.

By the end of this chapter, you will have a solid understanding of error handling and debugging in Bash scripting. You will be equipped with the tools and knowledge to handle errors gracefully, debug your scripts efficiently, and produce reliable and resilient code. Get ready to enhance the quality and reliability of your scripts through effective error handling and debugging techniques!

11.1 Handling Errors and Exceptions

Error handling is an important aspect of shell scripting to ensure that your scripts can gracefully handle unexpected situations and failures. This section explores techniques for handling errors and exceptions in Bash scripts.

1. Exit Status Codes:

In Bash, every command or program executed returns an exit status code, indicating whether the command executed successfully or encountered an error. The exit status code is stored in the special variable $?. Conventionally, an exit status code of 0 represents success, while non-zero codes indicate errors.

You can check the exit status code using conditional statements (if or case) to determine the success or failure of a command and take appropriate actions based on the result.

2. Error Handling Mechanisms:

There are several mechanisms available in Bash to handle errors and exceptions effectively:

Conditional Statements: Use if statements to check the exit status code and perform different actions based on success or failure. For example:

```
if command; then
   # Success
else
   # Failure
fi
```

Error Messages: Display informative error messages using the echo command or redirect error output (stderr) to a log file. This helps in diagnosing issues and provides meaningful feedback to users.

Error Codes and Logging: Assign specific error codes to different types of errors encountered in your script. This allows you to identify and handle errors more precisely. You can also log error messages and additional information to a log file for debugging purposes.

Error Handling Functions: Define error handling functions to centralize error handling logic. These functions can be called whenever an error is encountered, simplifying error handling code throughout your script.

Exit Traps: Use the trap command to set up exit traps that execute specific commands or functions before the script exits. This allows you to perform cleanup tasks, log errors, or perform other actions before terminating the script.

3. Error Reporting and Logging:

When handling errors, it's important to provide clear and informative error messages. This helps users understand the cause of the error and take appropriate actions. Consider including details such as the command that failed, the error code, and any relevant context information.

You can redirect error output (stderr) to a log file for better error logging and debugging. For example:

command 2>> error.log   # Redirect stderr to error.log

4. Graceful Script Termination:

In some cases, it may be necessary to terminate the script immediately upon encountering a critical error.

You can use the exit command to exit the script and optionally specify an exit status code. Additionally, the die or fatal functions can be defined to display an error message and terminate the script.

```
die() {
   echo "$@" >&2
   exit 1
}
```

Usage: die "Error message"

5. Try-Catch Blocks (Advanced):

Bash does not have built-in try-catch blocks like some other programming languages. However, you can emulate similar behavior by using functions and conditional statements. By encapsulating potentially error-prone code within a function and using conditional statements to handle errors, you can create a try-catch-like structure.

```
try {
   # Code that might encounter errors
}

catch {
   # Error handling logic
}
```

While not as straightforward as try-catch blocks in other languages, this approach can provide a structured way to handle errors within specific code sections.

Effective error handling is crucial for writing robust and reliable shell scripts. By incorporating error handling mechanisms, providing informative error messages, and gracefully terminating scripts when necessary, you can improve the resilience and maintainability of your Bash scripts.

11.2 Using Exit Codes and Error Messages

In Bash scripting, exit codes and error messages play a vital role in conveying the success or failure of commands and providing useful feedback to users. This section explores how to effectively use exit codes and error messages in your scripts.

1. Exit Codes:

Exit codes are integer values returned by commands and scripts, indicating the execution status. A zero (0) exit code typically signifies success, while non-zero codes indicate errors or specific conditions. By convention, different non-zero exit codes can be used to represent different types of errors or conditions.

To retrieve the exit code of the previously executed command, you can use the special variable $?. For example:

command
exit_code=$?

2. Using Exit Codes for Conditionals:

Exit codes are commonly used in conditional statements to determine the outcome of a command or script. You can use the if statement or the case statement to evaluate the exit code and perform appropriate actions based on success or failure.

For example, checking if a command succeeded:

if command; then
    # Command succeeded
else
    # Command failed
fi

Or checking specific exit codes using the case statement:

case $? in
   0)
      # Success
      ;;

```
    1)
        # Error code 1
        ;;
    *)
        # Other error codes
        ;;
esac
```

3. Error Messages:

Error messages provide valuable information about the cause of an error and assist users in understanding and resolving the issue. When an error occurs, it's important to display clear and meaningful error messages.

You can use the echo command to output error messages to the console or to an error log file. For example:

echo "An error occurred: Some error message" >&2 # Redirect to stderr

The >&2 notation redirects the output to the standard error stream instead of the standard output, ensuring that the error message is displayed appropriately.

4. Custom Error Codes:

In addition to the standard exit codes, you can define custom exit codes to represent specific error conditions in your script. This allows you to provide more granular information about the encountered errors. By documenting and consistently using custom error codes, you can make error handling more robust and informative.

For example, you can define custom error codes using variables:

ERR_INVALID_INPUT=10
ERR_FILE_NOT_FOUND=11

Usage: exit $ERR_INVALID_INPUT

5. Logging Errors:

Logging errors to a file can be useful for troubleshooting and debugging purposes. You can redirect the error messages to an error log file using the >> redirection operator. For example:

command >> error.log 2>&1   # Redirect stdout and stderr to error.log

This appends both the standard output and the standard error streams to the specified error log file.

6. Providing Guidance in Error Messages:

To assist users in resolving errors, consider providing guidance or suggestions in error messages. This can include instructions on how to rectify the issue, verify input data, or check system configurations. Helpful error messages can save time and effort for users and promote a better user experience.

By effectively utilizing exit codes and error messages, you can enhance the error handling capabilities of your Bash scripts. Clear and informative error messages help users understand and address issues, while exit codes provide a structured way to evaluate command execution. This combination enables better error handling and improves the overall reliability of your scripts.

11.3 Debugging Techniques and Tools

Debugging is an essential skill for shell script developers to identify and resolve issues in their scripts. This section explores various techniques and tools that can help you debug Bash scripts effectively.

1. Debugging Techniques:

Echo Statements: Inserting echo statements at strategic points in your script can help you understand the flow of execution and identify potential issues. By printing variable values, command outputs, or specific messages, you can track the script's progress and verify the expected behavior.

Logging: Logging relevant information, such as variable values, command outputs, or error messages, to a log file can assist in diagnosing issues. You can use the >> redirection operator to append log entries to a file throughout the script.

Verbose Mode: Invoking your script with the -v or --verbose option enables verbose mode, which displays each command before executing it. This can help you identify the specific command that causes an error or unexpected behavior.

Exit Traps: Setting up exit traps using the trap command allows you to execute custom commands or functions before the script exits. You can use this technique to capture the state of variables or perform cleanup tasks, providing additional insights into script execution.

Step-by-Step Execution: Temporarily modifying your script to execute one line or block of code at a time can help narrow down the source of errors. You can achieve this by commenting out portions of the script or using a debugger tool.

2. Debugging Tools:

Bash Debugging Mode (-x): Running your script with the -x option enables the Bash debugging mode. In this mode, each command is printed to the console with a + sign before execution. This allows you to trace the execution flow and identify problematic commands. For example:

bash -x script.sh

ShellCheck: ShellCheck is a static analysis tool that provides suggestions and warnings for shell scripts. It helps identify common coding issues, syntax errors, and potential pitfalls. You can run ShellCheck on your script either through the command-line interface or using online tools.

Debugging Frameworks: Several debugging frameworks and libraries are available for Bash scripting. These frameworks provide advanced debugging capabilities, such as breakpoints, variable inspection, and step-by-step execution. Examples include bashdb and bashdb2. Note that installing and setting up these frameworks may require additional effort.

3. Error Handling and Logging:

Effective error handling and logging practices can greatly facilitate the debugging process. By incorporating error messages, logging relevant information, and capturing error conditions, you can gain insights into the execution flow and pinpoint potential issues.

Error Messages: Display informative error messages using echo or printf statements to help identify the source of errors. Include relevant details, such as the command that failed, the error code, and any related variables or inputs.

Logging: Redirecting the standard output and standard error streams to log files allows you to capture and review script execution details. Logging variable values, command outputs, and error messages to the log file provides a comprehensive record for troubleshooting.

Verbose Mode and Debug Flags: Including options in your script to enable verbose mode or debug flags can provide additional information during execution. This can help in identifying the specific steps or commands causing issues.

Remember to remove or disable debugging statements and logging once you have resolved the issues to ensure your script runs efficiently.

Debugging is a valuable skill that allows you to identify and resolve issues in your Bash scripts effectively. By employing various debugging techniques, utilizing debugging tools, and incorporating robust error handling and logging practices, you can streamline the debugging process and produce reliable scripts.

Chapter 12: Advanced Shell Scripting Techniques

In this final chapter, we will explore advanced shell scripting techniques that will elevate your scripting skills to new heights. These techniques will enable you to tackle complex tasks, optimize performance, and unleash the full potential of shell scripting.

We will delve into advanced topics such as command-line arguments and options, allowing your scripts to accept input in a flexible and user-friendly manner. You will learn how to parse and process command-line arguments, handle flags and options, and incorporate them into your scripts effectively.

Next, we will explore regular expressions, a powerful tool for pattern matching and text manipulation. You will discover how to use regular expressions in your scripts to search for patterns, validate input, and perform advanced text processing operations.

Additionally, we will cover process management and job control, enabling you to manage multiple processes, create background tasks, and control process execution within your scripts. You will gain insights into process monitoring, signaling, and handling process exit codes.

Furthermore, we will touch upon scripting best practices, code optimization techniques, and shell scripting security considerations. You will learn how to write clean, efficient, and secure scripts that are maintainable and adhere to industry standards.

By mastering these advanced techniques, you will become a proficient and versatile shell scripter, capable of tackling complex scripting challenges and optimizing your workflow. Get ready to push the boundaries of shell scripting and unleash your creativity with advanced techniques in this exciting chapter!

12.1 Advanced Control Structures: select and until

In addition to the basic control structures like if-else and for loops, Bash provides some advanced control structures that offer increased flexibility in script execution. This section explores two such control structures: select and until.

1. The select Control Structure:

The select control structure is particularly useful when you want to present a menu-like interface to the user, allowing them to choose options from a list. It simplifies the process of handling user input and performing actions based on their selection. The basic syntax of the select structure is as follows:

```
select variable in option1 option2 option3 ...;
do
    # Actions based on the selected option
done
```

Here's a breakdown of how the select control structure works:

- The variable is the name of the variable that will store the user's selected option.
- The in keyword is used to specify the list of options from which the user can choose.
- The do keyword marks the beginning of the code block that will be executed for the selected option.
- Within the code block, you can perform actions based on the selected option.

Here's an example that demonstrates the usage of the select control structure:

```
select fruit in Apple Orange Banana;
do
    case $fruit in
        Apple)
            echo "You selected Apple."
            ;;
        Orange)
```

```
        echo "You selected Orange."
        ;;
     Banana)
        echo "You selected Banana."
        ;;
     *)
        echo "Invalid option. Please select again."
        ;;
   esac
done
```

In this example, the user is prompted to select a fruit from the provided options. Based on their selection, the corresponding message is displayed. If the user selects an invalid option, a message is shown, and the menu is presented again.

2. The until Control Structure:

The until control structure allows you to repeatedly execute a block of code until a certain condition is met. It is essentially the opposite of the while loop, as the code block is executed until the specified condition evaluates to true. The basic syntax of the until structure is as follows:

```
until condition;
do
    # Code to execute until the condition is true
done
```

Here's an example that demonstrates the usage of the until control structure:

```
count=0
until [ $count -ge 5 ];
do
   echo "Count: $count"
   ((count++))
done
```

In this example, the code block inside the until structure is executed until the condition $count -ge 5 (count greater than or equal to 5) becomes true. The value of the count variable is incremented in each iteration, and the current count is displayed.

The select and until control structures provide additional flexibility when designing Bash scripts. By leveraging the select structure, you can create interactive menus for user input, while the until structure allows you to repeat code execution until a specific condition is met. Understanding and utilizing these advanced control structures expands your scripting capabilities and enhances the user experience of your scripts.

12.2 Advanced String Manipulation and Regular Expressions

String manipulation and regular expressions are powerful techniques in Bash scripting that allow you to perform complex operations on text data. This section explores advanced string manipulation techniques and how to work with regular expressions in Bash.

1. Advanced String Manipulation:

Bash provides various built-in string manipulation features that enable you to manipulate and transform strings effectively. Here are some advanced techniques:

Substring Extraction: You can extract substrings from a larger string using the ${variable:offset:length} syntax. The offset represents the starting index of the substring, and the length specifies the number of characters to extract.

String Replacement: Bash offers the ${variable/pattern/replacement} syntax to replace the first occurrence of pattern with replacement within a string stored in the variable. Adding the /g flag at the end allows replacing all occurrences.

String Length: The ${#variable} syntax returns the length of a string stored in the variable.

String Concatenation: You can concatenate strings using the ${variable1}${variable2} syntax or by simply placing them together.

String Splitting: Bash provides the IFS (Internal Field Separator) variable to split strings into an array of substrings based on a delimiter. You can use the read command to read the delimited string into an array.

2. Regular Expressions:

Regular expressions (regex) are patterns used to match and manipulate text. Bash supports regex through various commands and operators, such as grep, sed, and the =~ operator. Here are some key regex concepts:

Character Classes: Character classes allow you to match specific sets of characters. For example, [a-zA-Z] matches any uppercase or lowercase letter.

Quantifiers: Quantifiers define the number of times a pattern or character should occur. Common quantifiers include * (zero or more occurrences), + (one or more occurrences), and ? (zero or one occurrence).

Anchors: Anchors are used to match patterns at specific positions within a string. The ^ anchor matches the start of a line, while the $ anchor matches the end of a line.

Grouping and Capturing: Parentheses () are used to group patterns together and capture specific portions of a matched string. The captured groups can be referenced later for substitution or further processing.

Escape Sequences: Escape sequences allow you to match special characters. For example, \. matches a literal period instead of interpreting it as a regex metacharacter.

Bash commands like grep and sed provide extensive regex support. You can use them to search for patterns, extract specific data, or perform substitutions in text files or command output.

Understanding advanced string manipulation techniques and regular expressions in Bash expands your ability to manipulate and process text data effectively. These techniques are particularly useful when working with complex string operations, pattern matching, and text processing tasks in your scripts.

12.3 Advanced File and Directory Operations

In addition to basic file and directory operations, Bash provides advanced features that allow you to perform complex operations on files and directories. This section explores some of these advanced file and directory operations.

1. File Permissions and Ownership:

Bash provides commands like chmod and chown to modify file permissions and ownership. With chmod, you can set permissions for a file or directory using symbolic or numeric notation. The symbolic notation includes letters like u (user), g (group), o (others), and a (all), along with operators like + (add permission), - (remove permission), and = (set exact permissions).

The chown command allows you to change the ownership of a file or directory, including the user and group ownership. This is particularly useful when you need to transfer ownership or restore permissions on specific files.

2. File and Directory Traversal:

Bash provides powerful techniques for traversing files and directories recursively. The find command is commonly used to search for files and directories based on various criteria, such as name, size, or permissions. It allows you to perform actions on the matched files, such as executing a command or applying further filters.

Another useful command is rsync, which enables efficient file and directory synchronization between different locations. It can be particularly helpful for backing up or transferring files, preserving permissions, and handling incremental updates.

3. File Compression and Archiving:

Bash offers several commands for file compression and archiving, such as gzip, tar, and zip. gzip is used to compress individual files, creating .gz compressed files. tar allows you to create archives of multiple files and directories, which can be further compressed using gzip or other compression algorithms.

The zip command is commonly used for creating ZIP archives, which are widely supported across different platforms. It provides options to encrypt archives and compress files while preserving the directory structure.

4. File Comparison and Diff:

Bash provides tools for comparing and finding differences between files. The diff command compares two files line by line, highlighting the differences. It can be useful for detecting changes in configuration files or tracking modifications in source code.

The cmp command compares two files byte by byte and reports the first differing byte's position. This is particularly useful when comparing binary files or verifying the integrity of files.

5. File Permissions and Attributes:

Bash provides commands like stat and lsattr to retrieve information about file permissions and attributes. stat displays detailed information about a file or directory, including access rights, size, modification time, and more.

The lsattr command lists file attributes, such as the immutable flag or the append-only flag. These attributes can be used to enhance file security and prevent accidental modifications.

Understanding these advanced file and directory operations allows you to perform more sophisticated tasks in your Bash scripts. Whether it's managing permissions, navigating complex directory structures, or performing file comparisons, leveraging these advanced features expands your ability to handle file and directory operations efficiently.

12.4 Advanced Scripting Tools and Utilities

When it comes to advanced shell scripting, having knowledge of various tools and utilities can greatly enhance your productivity and the functionality of your scripts. This section introduces some popular advanced scripting tools and utilities that can be used in conjunction with Bash.

1. AWK:

AWK is a powerful text-processing language that allows you to manipulate and analyze structured text data. It excels at working with columns and fields in text files, making it a valuable tool for data extraction, formatting, and reporting. AWK provides a wide range of built-in functions and supports custom scripting logic using pattern-action pairs.

2. sed:

sed (stream editor) is a command-line utility designed for text manipulation. It operates on a line-by-line basis, allowing you to perform search and replace operations, insert or delete lines, apply regular expressions, and more. sed is often used for batch editing of files, transforming text, and streamlining data processing tasks.

3. grep:

grep is a versatile command-line tool for searching text patterns in files or command output. It supports regular expressions and provides various options for controlling the search behavior. grep can be used to find specific lines matching a pattern, count occurrences, exclude certain patterns, and search recursively in directories.

4. find:

The find command is a powerful tool for searching files and directories based on various criteria. It allows you to locate files by name, size, type, modification time, and other attributes. You can combine find with other commands to perform actions on the matched files, such as executing scripts or applying modifications.

5. xargs:

xargs is a command-line utility that takes input from standard input (or files) and converts it into arguments for another command. It is useful when you need to process a large number of files or perform operations on multiple items at once. xargs allows you to control how the input is split and passed as arguments to the subsequent command.

6. jq:

jq is a lightweight and flexible command-line tool for processing JSON data. It provides a simple and expressive syntax to extract, manipulate, and transform JSON structures. With jq, you can filter and query JSON data, perform calculations, apply conditional logic, and create JSON output.

7. parallel:

parallel is a command-line tool that allows you to run commands in parallel, maximizing the utilization of available resources. It is particularly useful when dealing with computationally intensive tasks or when you need to process multiple files simultaneously. parallel splits the input data and distributes the workload across multiple cores or machines.

By familiarizing yourself with these advanced scripting tools and utilities, you can leverage their capabilities to handle complex tasks efficiently. Each tool serves a specific purpose, enabling you to streamline text processing, file manipulation, data extraction, and parallel execution within your Bash scripts.

Chapter 13: Working with Command-Line Arguments

Command-line arguments provide a powerful means of customizing the behavior of your scripts at runtime. In this chapter, we will explore the techniques for effectively working with command-line arguments in your shell scripts.

We will begin by understanding how to read and access command-line arguments within your scripts. You will learn how to extract and process individual arguments, handle flags and options, and validate the input provided by users.

Next, we will dive into advanced command-line argument parsing techniques, such as using the getopts utility, which allows you to handle complex options and provide a more intuitive user experience. You will gain insights into handling short and long options, specifying required and optional arguments, and providing usage instructions.

Furthermore, we will explore strategies for error handling and input validation when working with command-line arguments. You will learn how to handle missing or invalid arguments, provide meaningful error messages, and gracefully guide users in providing the correct input.

By the end of this chapter, you will have a solid understanding of how to work with command-line arguments in your shell scripts. You will be able to create scripts that are flexible, customizable, and user-friendly, enabling users to tailor the script's behavior to their specific needs. Get ready to harness the power of command-line arguments and enhance the versatility of your shell scripts!

13.1 Introduction to Command-Line Arguments

Command-line arguments are a powerful feature in shell scripting that allow you to pass values or options to a script when it is executed. They provide a convenient way to customize the behavior of a script without modifying its code. This section introduces the concept of command-line arguments and how to work with them in your shell scripts.

Understanding Command-Line Arguments:

Command-line arguments are additional values or options passed to a script when it is invoked from the command line. They allow users to provide inputs or instructions to the script at runtime. For example, if you have a script called "my_script.sh," you can execute it with command-line arguments like this:

```
$ ./my_script.sh arg1 arg2 arg3
```

In this example, "arg1," "arg2," and "arg3" are the command-line arguments passed to the script. The script can access and utilize these values during its execution.

Accessing Command-Line Arguments:

In Bash, command-line arguments are stored in special variables. The primary variable is $1, which represents the first command-line argument. The second argument is stored in $2, the third in $3, and so on. To access the command-line arguments within your script, you can reference these variables.

For example, consider the following script:

```
#!/bin/bash

echo "The first argument is: $1"
echo "The second argument is: $2"
echo "The third argument is: $3"
```

If you execute this script with command-line arguments, it will display the corresponding values:

```
$ ./my_script.sh value1 value2 value3
The first argument is: value1
The second argument is: value2
The third argument is: value3
```

Handling Variable Number of Arguments:

In some cases, you may want to handle a variable number of command-line arguments. Bash provides the special variable $@, which represents all the command-line arguments as a list. You can iterate over this list using a loop or access specific arguments by their index.

#!/bin/bash

echo "Total number of arguments: $#"

Loop through all arguments
echo "All arguments:"
for arg in "$@"; do
    echo "$arg"
done

In this example, $# represents the total number of command-line arguments. The loop iterates over all the arguments using "$@", and each argument is printed.

Using Command-Line Options:

In addition to passing values as arguments, you can also use command-line options or flags to modify the behavior of your script. Command-line options are typically preceded by a hyphen (-) or double hyphen

(--). For example, you might have an option -v to enable verbose output or --help to display a help message.

To handle command-line options, you can use the getopts command in Bash. It allows you to define and parse options, set default values, and perform actions based on the provided options.

```bash
#!/bin/bash

# Define options
while getopts "vho:" opt; do
   case $opt in
      v)
         echo "Verbose mode enabled"
         ;;
      h)
         echo "Help message:"
         echo "..."
         ;;
      o)
         echo "Output file: $OPTARG"
         ;;
      *)
         echo "Invalid option: $opt"
         ;;
   esac
done
```

In this example, the script defines three options: -v for verbose mode, -h for displaying a help message, and -o for specifying an output file. The getopts command is used to handle these options and execute the corresponding actions.

Command-line arguments provide a flexible way to interact with your scripts and make them more versatile. By leveraging command-line arguments, you can create scripts that accept inputs, options, and configurations from users, allowing for greater customization and adaptability.

13.2 Parsing and Validating Command-Line Arguments

When working with command-line arguments in shell scripting, it's essential to properly parse and validate the input to ensure that it meets the expected format and requirements. This section explores techniques for parsing and validating command-line arguments to enhance the robustness and reliability of your scripts.

Parsing Command-Line Arguments:

Parsing command-line arguments involves extracting values or options from the provided arguments and assigning them to variables within your script. One common approach is to use the getopts command in

Bash, which simplifies the parsing process and handles options and their arguments.

Here's an example of how to use getopts to parse command-line options and their arguments:

```bash
#!/bin/bash

while getopts ":a:b:c:" opt; do
  case $opt in
    a)
      arg1="$OPTARG"
      ;;
    b)
      arg2="$OPTARG"
      ;;
    c)
      arg3="$OPTARG"
      ;;
    \?)
      echo "Invalid option: -$OPTARG"
      ;;
  esac
done

echo "Argument 1: $arg1"
echo "Argument 2: $arg2"
echo "Argument 3: $arg3"
```

In this example, the script expects three options: -a, -b, and -c. The corresponding arguments for these options are stored in the variables arg1, arg2, and arg3. The : in the getopts options string indicates that these options require arguments.

Validating Command-Line Arguments:

Validating command-line arguments ensures that they meet certain criteria or constraints defined by your script. Here are some common techniques for validating command-line arguments:

Checking the number of arguments: You can verify that the correct number of arguments is provided by comparing $# (the number of arguments) with the expected count.

Checking argument values: You can validate individual argument values using conditional statements. For example, you can check if an argument is a valid file path, a numeric value, or falls within a specific range.

Using regular expressions: Regular expressions provide a powerful tool for validating argument values against specific patterns. You can use tools like grep or the =~ operator in Bash to match argument values against regular expressions.

Handling default values: If certain arguments are optional, you can set default values for them. This ensures that the script can still execute even if those arguments are not provided.

Here's an example that demonstrates validating command-line arguments:

```bash
#!/bin/bash

if [ $# -ne 2 ]; then
  echo "Usage: ./script.sh <username> <password>"
  exit 1
fi

username=$1
password=$2

# Validating username
if [[ ! $username =~ ^[a-zA-Z0-9_]+$ ]]; then
  echo "Invalid username"
  exit 1
fi

# Validating password length
if [ ${#password} -lt 8 ]; then
  echo "Password must be at least 8 characters long"
  exit 1
fi

echo "Username: $username"
echo "Password: $password"
```

In this example, the script expects two arguments: a username and a password. It validates the arguments by checking their length and pattern. If any validation fails, an error message is displayed, and the script exits.

By properly parsing and validating command-line arguments, you can ensure that your script receives the expected input and gracefully handle any errors or incorrect usage. This helps create more robust and reliable shell scripts.

13.3 Advanced Command-Line Argument Handling

In addition to basic parsing and validation, there are advanced techniques you can employ to enhance the handling of command-line arguments in your shell scripts. This section explores some of these techniques, including optional arguments, flags, and argument grouping.

Optional Arguments:

While mandatory arguments are essential for your script's functionality, there may be cases where you want to provide optional arguments that modify or customize the script's behavior. To handle optional arguments, you can use the getopts command and assign default values when an optional argument is not provided.

```bash
#!/bin/bash

while getopts ":f:o:" opt; do
  case $opt in
    f)
      file="$OPTARG"
      ;;
    o)
      output="$OPTARG"
      ;;
    \?)
      echo "Invalid option: -$OPTARG"
      ;;
  esac
done

# Set default values for optional arguments
file=${file:-"input.txt"}
output=${output:-"output.txt"}

echo "Input file: $file"
echo "Output file: $output"
```

In this example, the script expects two optional arguments: -f for the input file and -o for the output file. If these arguments are not provided, default values are assigned. This allows users to omit optional arguments while still ensuring the script executes correctly.

Flags:

Flags, also known as boolean options, are command-line arguments that indicate the presence or absence of a specific feature or behavior. Flags are typically used to enable or disable certain functionalities within your script. You can handle flags by using a variable to store their state, such as true or false.

```
#!/bin/bash

verbose=false

while getopts ":v" opt; do
  case $opt in
    v)
      verbose=true
      ;;
    \?)
      echo "Invalid option: -$OPTARG"
      ;;
  esac
done

if $verbose; then
  echo "Verbose mode enabled"
else
```

```
  echo "Verbose mode disabled"
fi
```

In this example, the script expects a flag -v to enable verbose mode. If the flag is present, the verbose variable is set to true, indicating that verbose mode is enabled. Otherwise, it is set to false.

Argument Grouping:

Sometimes, you may want to group related arguments together for convenience and clarity. This can be achieved by using subcommands or suboptions. For example, consider a script that performs various actions related to user management: ./user_management.sh add, ./user_management.sh delete, and so on.

```
#!/bin/bash

case $1 in
  add)
    # Code for adding a user
    ;;
  delete)
    # Code for deleting a user
    ;;
  update)
    # Code for updating a user
    ;;
  *)
```

```
        echo "Invalid command: $1"
        ;;
esac
```

In this example, the script takes a subcommand as the first argument (add, delete, update) to determine the specific action to perform. Each subcommand can have its own set of arguments or options, allowing for better organization and clarity in your script.

By employing techniques like optional arguments, flags, and argument grouping, you can create more flexible and user-friendly shell scripts. These advanced command-line argument handling techniques provide greater control and customization options to your script's users.

Chapter 14: Working with Regular Expressions

Regular expressions are a powerful tool for pattern matching and text manipulation in shell scripting. In this chapter, we will dive into the world of regular expressions and explore how they can enhance your scripting capabilities.

We will start by understanding the fundamentals of regular expressions, including metacharacters, character classes, quantifiers, and anchors. You will learn how to construct and use regular expressions to match patterns in strings and perform advanced text manipulation operations.

Next, we will explore how to incorporate regular expressions into your shell scripts. You will discover how to use tools like grep, sed, and awk to leverage the power of regular expressions for searching, filtering, and transforming text data. We will cover advanced techniques such as capturing groups, backreferences, and lookahead/lookbehind assertions.

Additionally, we will discuss how to handle common scenarios like escaping special characters, handling multiline text, and performing case-insensitive matching. You will gain insights into the nuances of regular expressions in shell scripting and learn how to overcome challenges that may arise.

By the end of this chapter, you will have a solid understanding of regular expressions and how to effectively use them in your shell scripts. You will be able to create robust scripts that can handle complex text patterns, perform advanced text manipulation operations, and extract valuable information from your data. Get ready to master the art of working with regular expressions in shell scripting!

14.1 Introduction to Regular Expressions

Regular expressions (regex) are powerful tools for pattern matching and manipulating text. They provide a concise and flexible way to search, extract, and manipulate strings based on specific patterns. Regular expressions are widely used in shell scripting for tasks such as data validation, text parsing, and pattern matching. This chapter introduces the basics of regular expressions and their usage in shell scripting.

What is a Regular Expression?

A regular expression is a sequence of characters that forms a search pattern. It consists of literal characters (such as letters, digits, and symbols) and metacharacters, which have special meanings. Metacharacters allow you to define complex patterns by representing classes of characters, repetitions, alternations, and more.

Common Metacharacters:

Here are some commonly used metacharacters in regular expressions:

- . (dot): Matches any single character except a newline.
- * (asterisk): Matches zero or more occurrences of the preceding character or group.
- + (plus): Matches one or more occurrences of the preceding character or group.
- ? (question mark): Matches zero or one occurrence of the preceding character or group.
- [] (square brackets): Defines a character class, matching any single character within the brackets.
- () (parentheses): Groups characters or expressions together.

Basic Pattern Matching:

To perform pattern matching using regular expressions in shell scripting, you can use tools like grep, sed, or the =~ operator in Bash. These tools allow you to search for patterns in text and perform actions based on the matching results.

Here's an example that demonstrates basic pattern matching using grep:

#!/bin/bash

Search for lines containing "apple" in a file
grep "apple" file.txt

In this example, grep "apple" searches for lines in the file file.txt that contain the word "apple". It returns all matching lines.

Character Classes:

Character classes allow you to define sets or ranges of characters to match. They are enclosed in square brackets [] and can include individual characters, character ranges, or predefined character classes.

Here are some examples of character classes:

- [abc]: Matches any of the characters a, b, or c.
- [0-9]: Matches any digit from 0 to 9.
- [a-zA-Z]: Matches any uppercase or lowercase letter.
- [[:digit:]]: Matches any digit (same as [0-9]).
- [[:alpha:]]: Matches any alphabetic character.

Anchors and Boundaries:

Anchors and boundaries are used to match specific positions within a string. They do not match any actual characters but rather positions in the string.

- ^ (caret): Matches the start of a line.
- $ (dollar sign): Matches the end of a line.
- \b (word boundary): Matches the boundary between a word character and a non-word character.
- \B (non-word boundary): Matches the position that is not a word boundary.

Quantifiers:

Quantifiers specify the number of occurrences of a character or group that should be matched.

- *: Matches zero or more occurrences.
- +: Matches one or more occurrences.
- ?: Matches zero or one occurrence.
- {n}: Matches exactly n occurrences.
- {n,}: Matches at least n occurrences.
- {n,m}: Matches between n and m occurrences.

Regular expressions provide a rich set of features and syntax for pattern matching and manipulation. By mastering regular expressions, you can effectively process and transform text data in your shell scripts.

14.2 Pattern Matching and Regular Expression Operators

In shell scripting, pattern matching and regular expressions are powerful tools for searching, manipulating, and validating text data. Various operators and constructs are available to work with regular expressions, enabling you to perform complex pattern matching operations. This section explores some common operators and constructs used for pattern matching in shell scripts.

The =~ Operator:

The =~ operator is used in Bash to match a string against a regular expression. It allows you to check if a string matches a specified pattern. Here's an example:

```
#!/bin/bash

string="Hello, World!"

if [[ $string =~ "Hello" ]]; then
  echo "Match found"
else
  echo "No match"
fi
```

In this example, the =~ operator is used to check if the variable string contains the substring "Hello". If it does, the script prints "Match found". Otherwise, it prints "No match".

Anchors:

Anchors are regular expression constructs used to specify the position of a pattern within a string. The most commonly used anchors are the caret ^ and the dollar sign $.

- ^ (caret) matches the start of a line or string.
- $ (dollar sign) matches the end of a line or string.

Here's an example that demonstrates the usage of anchors:

```
#!/bin/bash

string="Hello, World!"

if [[ $string =~ "^Hello" ]]; then
  echo "Starts with Hello"
fi

if [[ $string =~ "World!$" ]]; then
  echo "Ends with World!"
fi
```

In this example, the first if statement checks if the variable string starts with "Hello", and the second if statement checks if it ends with "World!". If the conditions are met, the corresponding messages are printed.

Character Classes:

Character classes allow you to define sets or ranges of characters to match. They are enclosed in square brackets [] and can include individual characters, character ranges, or predefined character classes.

Here's an example that uses character classes to match specific characters:

```
#!/bin/bash

string="The quick brown fox jumps over the lazy dog."

if [[ $string =~ [aeiou] ]]; then
  echo "Vowel found"
fi

if [[ $string =~ [a-z] ]]; then
  echo "Lowercase letter found"
fi
```

In this example, the first if statement checks if the variable string contains any vowel character, and the second if statement checks if it contains any lowercase letter. If a match is found, the corresponding messages are printed.

Quantifiers:

Quantifiers specify the number of occurrences of a character or group that should be matched.

- * matches zero or more occurrences.
- + matches one or more occurrences.
- ? matches zero or one occurrence.
- {n} matches exactly n occurrences.
- {n,} matches at least n occurrences.
- {n,m} matches between n and m occurrences.

Here's an example that demonstrates the usage of quantifiers:

```
#!/bin/bash

string="Helloooo!"

if [[ $string =~ o{3,} ]]; then
    echo "Three or more consecutive 'o' characters found"
fi
```

In this example, the script checks if the variable string contains three or more consecutive "o" characters. If a match is found, the corresponding message is printed.

Regular expression operators and constructs provide powerful ways to work with patterns in shell scripting. By understanding and utilizing these operators, you can perform advanced pattern matching operations in your scripts.

14.3 Using Regular Expressions in Bash Scripts

Regular expressions are widely used in Bash scripts for pattern matching, text manipulation, and data validation. They provide a flexible and powerful way to search, extract, and manipulate text based on specific patterns. This section explores how regular expressions can be used effectively in Bash scripts.

Pattern Matching with grep:

The grep command is commonly used to search for patterns in text files or the output of other commands. It allows you to specify a regular expression pattern and search for lines that match that pattern. Here's an example:

```
#!/bin/bash

# Search for lines starting with "Error"
grep "^Error" log.txt
```

In this example, the grep command searches for lines in the file log.txt that start with the word "Error". It returns all matching lines.

Pattern Replacement with sed:

The sed command is a stream editor that can perform various operations on text, including pattern replacement. It allows you to specify a regular expression pattern and replace it with a desired string. Here's an example:

#!/bin/bash

Replace all occurrences of "apple" with "orange"
sed 's/apple/orange/g' fruits.txt

In this example, the sed command replaces all occurrences of the word "apple" with "orange" in the file fruits.txt. The s/apple/orange/g expression is a regular expression pattern substitution command.

Pattern Matching and Extraction with Capture Groups:

Regular expressions can also be used to extract specific parts of a string by using capture groups. Capture groups are portions of a regular expression enclosed in parentheses () that define a subpattern. Here's an example:

```bash
#!/bin/bash

# Extract the date from a log entry
log_entry="2023-06-20 14:30:45 [INFO] Task completed successfully"
regex="([0-9]{4}-[0-9]{2}-[0-9]{2})"

if [[ $log_entry =~ $regex ]]; then
  extracted_date="${BASH_REMATCH[1]}"
  echo "Extracted date: $extracted_date"
fi
```

In this example, the script extracts the date portion from a log entry. The regular expression pattern ([0-9]{4}-[0-9]{2}-[0-9]{2}) matches a date in the format "YYYY-MM-DD". The captured date is stored in the BASH_REMATCH array, and it is then printed.

Data Validation with Pattern Matching:

Regular expressions are useful for validating user input or verifying data formats. They allow you to enforce specific patterns and validate input against those patterns. Here's an example of validating an email address:

```bash
#!/bin/bash

read -p "Enter your email address: " email
```

```
regex="^[A-Za-z0-9._%+-]+@[A-Za-z0-9.-]+\.[A-Za-z]{2,}$"

if [[ $email =~ $regex ]]; then
  echo "Email address is valid"
else
  echo "Invalid email address"
fi
```

In this example, the script prompts the user to enter an email address. The regular expression pattern ^[A-Za-z0-9._%+-]+@[A-Za-z0-9.-]+\.[A-Za-z]{2,}$ validates the email address format. If the input matches the pattern, it is considered valid; otherwise, it is considered invalid.

Regular expressions provide a versatile and powerful toolset for pattern matching and text manipulation in Bash scripts. By using them effectively, you can enhance the functionality and flexibility of your scripts.

Chapter 15: Process Management and Job Control

Process management and job control are essential aspects of shell scripting, allowing you to handle multiple processes, manage their execution, and optimize your script's performance. In this chapter, we will explore the techniques for effective process management and job control in your shell scripts.

We will begin by understanding the basics of process management, including launching and terminating processes, monitoring their status, and retrieving process IDs (PIDs). You will learn how to use commands such as ps, kill, and pgrep to interact with processes within your scripts.

Next, we will delve into job control, which enables you to manage multiple processes simultaneously. You will discover how to run processes in the background, bring them to the foreground, and control their execution using signals and job control commands.

Furthermore, we will explore techniques for process synchronization, allowing you to coordinate the execution of multiple processes and ensure they run in a desired order. You will learn about locking mechanisms, inter-process communication (IPC), and techniques like semaphores and signals for process coordination.

Additionally, we will discuss process monitoring and error handling strategies. You will learn how to capture and handle process exit codes, log process activities, and implement error handling mechanisms to ensure the robustness and reliability of your scripts.

By the end of this chapter, you will have a solid understanding of process management and job control techniques in shell scripting. You will be equipped with the skills to manage and coordinate processes effectively, optimize performance, and create resilient scripts that handle multiple tasks seamlessly. Get ready to take control of your processes and master the art of process management and job control in your shell scripts!

15.1 Managing Processes in Bash

In Bash scripting, managing processes is an important aspect of automating tasks and controlling the execution of commands. Understanding how to interact with processes allows you to monitor and control their behavior. This section explores various techniques for managing processes in Bash.

Running Background Processes:

By default, when you execute a command or script in Bash, it runs in the foreground, occupying the terminal until it completes. However, you can run processes in the background, allowing them to execute independently while you continue to use the terminal. To run a process in the background, you can append an ampersand & to the end of the command. Here's an example:

```
#!/bin/bash

# Run a long-running command in the background
sleep 10 &
echo "Process running in the background"
```

In this example, the sleep 10 command is executed in the background using &. The script immediately proceeds to the next line and prints "Process running in the background" without waiting for the sleep command to complete.

Listing Running Processes:

To obtain information about currently running processes, you can use the ps command. It allows you to list processes and retrieve details such as the process ID (PID), CPU and memory usage, and the command associated with each process. Here's an example:

```
#!/bin/bash

# List all running processes
```

ps aux

In this example, the ps aux command lists all running processes and displays information about each process.

Killing Processes:

To terminate a running process, you can use the kill command followed by the process ID (PID). The kill command sends a signal to the specified process, instructing it to terminate. Here's an example:

#!/bin/bash

```
# Terminate a specific process
process_id=12345
kill $process_id
```

In this example, the kill command is used to terminate the process with the ID 12345.

Process Monitoring:

You can monitor the status and behavior of a running process using tools like top, htop, or ps. These tools provide real-time information about CPU usage, memory consumption, and other metrics. Here's an example using the top command:

#!/bin/bash

```
# Monitor CPU usage using top
top
```

In this example, the top command displays an interactive view showing the current state of running processes, sorted by CPU usage. You can press q to exit top.

Process Control:

Bash provides built-in mechanisms for controlling the execution of processes within a script. For example, you can use the wait command to wait for the completion of background processes before proceeding with the script. Here's an example:

```
#!/bin/bash

# Run two processes in the background
sleep 5 &
sleep 10 &

# Wait for all background processes to complete
wait

echo "All background processes have completed"
```

In this example, two sleep commands are executed in the background. The wait command ensures that the script waits for both background processes to complete before continuing.

Managing processes in Bash allows you to run tasks concurrently, monitor their progress, and control their execution. By leveraging these techniques, you can automate complex workflows and improve the efficiency of your scripts.

15.2 Background and Foreground Processes

In Bash scripting, you can run processes either in the foreground or in the background. Understanding the differences between background and foreground processes is essential for managing and controlling the execution of commands. This section explores the concepts of background and foreground processes and how to work with them in Bash.

Foreground Processes:

By default, when you execute a command or script in Bash, it runs in the foreground. Foreground processes take control of the terminal, and the shell waits for them to complete before allowing further input or executing subsequent commands. For example:

#!/bin/bash

```
# Run a long-running command in the foreground
sleep 10
echo "Foreground process completed"
```

In this example, the sleep 10 command runs in the foreground, occupying the terminal for 10 seconds. After the command completes, the script proceeds to the next line and prints "Foreground process completed".

Background Processes:

In contrast, background processes run independently of the terminal, allowing you to continue using the terminal for other tasks while the process is running. You can execute a process in the background by appending an ampersand & to the end of the command. For example:

```
#!/bin/bash

# Run a long-running command in the background
sleep 10 &
echo "Background process started"
```

In this example, the sleep 10 command runs in the background, and the script immediately proceeds to the next line without waiting for the command to complete. The message "Background process started" is printed immediately.

Managing Background Processes:

When you execute a process in the background, Bash assigns it a unique process ID (PID) and allows it to run independently. You can manage background processes using various commands and techniques:

- **jobs**: The jobs command lists all currently running or suspended background jobs in the current shell session. It displays the job ID and status of each background process.
- **fg**: The fg command brings a background process to the foreground, allowing you to interact with it as if it were running in the foreground.
- **bg**: The bg command resumes a suspended background process and allows it to continue running.
- **kill**: The kill command can be used to send a signal to a background process, such as terminating or stopping it.

Here's an example demonstrating the use of jobs, fg, and bg commands:

#!/bin/bash

Run a long-running command in the background

```
sleep 10 &

# List background jobs
jobs

# Bring the background process to the foreground
fg %1

# Suspend the foreground process
Ctrl + Z

# List background jobs again
jobs

# Resume the suspended background process
bg %1
```

In this example, the sleep 10 command is executed in the background. The jobs command lists the background job, and fg %1 brings the background process to the foreground. Pressing Ctrl + Z suspends the foreground process, and bg %1 resumes it in the background.

Working with background and foreground processes gives you flexibility in managing tasks in Bash scripts. By running processes in the background, you can free up the terminal for other operations and automate complex workflows effectively.

15.3 Job Control and Process Monitoring

In Bash scripting, job control and process monitoring are essential for managing and monitoring the execution of commands and scripts. Job control allows you to manipulate and control the behavior of running processes, while process monitoring provides real-time information about the state and performance of processes. This section explores the concepts of job control and process monitoring in Bash.

Job Control:

Job control in Bash provides mechanisms for managing and manipulating running processes. It allows you to:

- **Foreground and Background Execution**: You can move a process between the foreground and background using the fg and bg commands. The fg command brings a background process to the foreground, while the bg command resumes a suspended or stopped process in the background.
- **Suspend and Resume Execution**: You can suspend the execution of a foreground process using Ctrl + Z and resume it in the foreground or background using the fg or bg commands.

- **Termination and Killing**: The Ctrl + C key combination sends an interrupt signal (SIGINT) to the foreground process, terminating it. You can use the kill command to send other signals to a process, such as termination (SIGTERM) or a forced termination (SIGKILL).

Here's an example demonstrating the use of job control:

```bash
#!/bin/bash

# Run a long-running command in the foreground
sleep 10

# Run another command in the background
command &

# Suspend the foreground process
Ctrl + Z

# List all jobs
jobs

# Bring the background job to the foreground
fg %1

# Terminate the foreground job
Ctrl + C
```

In this example, the sleep 10 command runs in the foreground. The command & runs another command in the background. Pressing Ctrl + Z suspends the foreground process, and the jobs command lists all jobs. The fg %1 brings the background job to the foreground, and Ctrl + C terminates the foreground job.

Process Monitoring:

Process monitoring allows you to gather real-time information about running processes, such as CPU usage, memory consumption, and other metrics. Bash provides various tools for process monitoring, including:

- **top**: The top command displays an interactive view of running processes, sorted by CPU usage. It provides real-time updates and detailed information about each process.
- **ps**: The ps command lists running processes and provides detailed information, such as process ID (PID), CPU and memory usage, and associated command.
- **htop**: The htop command is an enhanced version of top, providing a more user-friendly and interactive process monitoring experience.

Here's an example using the top command for process monitoring:

```
#!/bin/bash

# Monitor CPU usage using top
top
```

In this example, the top command displays an interactive view showing the current state of running processes, sorted by CPU usage. Press q to exit top.

By utilizing job control and process monitoring techniques, you can effectively manage and monitor the execution of commands and scripts in Bash. These capabilities provide flexibility and control over running processes, allowing you to automate complex tasks and optimize system performance.

Chapter 16: Shell Scripting Best Practices

In this final chapter, we will explore the best practices for writing efficient, maintainable, and secure shell scripts. Adopting these practices will enhance the quality of your scripts, promote code readability, and minimize potential errors or vulnerabilities.

We will start by discussing the importance of script documentation and providing clear and concise comments. You will learn how to document your scripts effectively, including script purpose, input requirements, output expectations, and any dependencies or prerequisites.

Next, we will cover code organization and structure. You will discover techniques for breaking down your script into modular functions, organizing variables and constants, and adopting a logical flow within your script. These practices will improve code maintainability and make your scripts easier to understand and debug.

Furthermore, we will explore error handling and graceful script termination. You will learn how to handle errors appropriately, display meaningful error messages to users, and implement fallback strategies to handle unexpected situations gracefully.

Additionally, we will discuss shell scripting security considerations. You will gain insights into preventing common vulnerabilities, such as input validation, proper handling of user input, and securing sensitive data within your scripts.

Moreover, we will touch upon performance optimization techniques. You will learn how to minimize resource usage, optimize loops and iterations, and employ efficient data processing techniques to improve the performance of your scripts.

By following these best practices, you will be able to create high-quality shell scripts that are easy to maintain, secure, and performant. Your scripts will become reliable tools that deliver consistent and accurate results. Get ready to elevate your scripting skills and produce professional-grade shell scripts through the adoption of best practices!

16.1 Writing Clear and Readable Code

When it comes to shell scripting, writing clear and readable code is crucial for several reasons. It improves code maintainability, enhances collaboration with other developers, and reduces the likelihood of introducing errors. In this chapter, we will explore various techniques and best practices for writing clear and readable shell scripts.

1. Use Meaningful Variable Names:

Choose descriptive names for your variables that convey their purpose. Avoid single-letter variable names or cryptic abbreviations that may confuse readers. For example:

```
# Bad
a="1"
b="hello"

# Good
count="1"
message="hello"
```

2. Indentation and Formatting:

Indent your code consistently to improve readability. Use spaces for indentation rather than tabs, and choose a consistent number of spaces for each level of indentation (e.g., 2 or 4 spaces). Properly format your code by aligning related elements. For example:

```
# Bad
if [ "$count" -eq 10 ]; then
echo "Count is 10"
else
echo "Count is not 10"
fi
```

```
# Good
if [ "$count" -eq 10 ]; then
  echo "Count is 10"
else
  echo "Count is not 10"
fi
```

3. Use Comments:

Comments provide additional context and explanations within your code. Use comments to describe the purpose of complex sections, clarify any potential confusion, or document your code's behavior. However, avoid excessive commenting for self-evident code. For example:

```
# Bad
# Increment count by 1
count=$((count + 1))
```

```
# Good
count=$((count + 1))  # Increment count by 1
```

4. Break Down Complex Logic:

Avoid writing long, monolithic scripts. Break down complex tasks into smaller functions or separate sections to improve readability and maintainability. Each function or section should have a clear purpose and perform a specific task. For example:

```
# Bad
# Complex logic with multiple tasks

# Good
function task1() {
  # Task 1 logic
}

function task2() {
  # Task 2 logic
}

# Main script
task1
task2
```

5. Error Handling and Robustness:

Include error handling mechanisms in your code to ensure proper handling of unexpected conditions and failures. Use appropriate error codes, error messages, and logging to provide useful information to users or developers encountering issues. For example:

```
# Bad
command1
command2
command3

# Good
```

```
if ! command1; then
  echo "Error: Command 1 failed"
  exit 1
fi

if ! command2; then
  echo "Error: Command 2 failed"
  exit 1
fi

if ! command3; then
  echo "Error: Command 3 failed"
  exit 1
fi
```

6. Follow Naming Conventions:

Adhere to common naming conventions to make your code more understandable and consistent. For example, use uppercase letters for constants and lowercase letters for variables and functions. Choose a naming style and stick to it throughout your script. For example:

```
# Constants
readonly MAX_COUNT=10

# Variables
count=0

# Functions
```

```
my_function() {
  # Function logic
}
```

Writing clear and readable code in your shell scripts not only benefits you but also makes it easier for others to understand, maintain, and collaborate on your code. By following these practices, you can enhance the quality and readability of your shell scripts.

16.2 Handling Errors and Exceptions Properly

Handling errors and exceptions effectively is crucial in shell scripting to ensure robust and reliable code. By implementing proper error handling techniques, you can anticipate and respond to unexpected conditions, prevent script failures, and provide meaningful feedback to users. In this chapter, we will explore various approaches for handling errors and exceptions in shell scripts.

1. Exit on Error:

Set the errexit option (-e) at the beginning of your script to ensure that any command returning a non-zero exit status immediately terminates the script.

This helps prevent the script from continuing execution in an inconsistent state. For example:

```
#!/bin/bash

set -e

# Command 1
command1

# Command 2
command2

# Command 3
command3
```

If any of the commands command1, command2, or command3 fail, the script will exit immediately.

2. Conditional Error Handling:

Use conditional statements and error-checking constructs, such as if statements or command substitution, to handle errors selectively. This allows you to perform specific actions based on the success or failure of a command. For example:

```
#!/bin/bash

# Run a command and check the exit status
if command1; then
```

```
  echo "Command 1 succeeded"
else
  echo "Command 1 failed"
fi
```

You can also utilize the && and || operators to execute commands conditionally based on their success or failure. For example:

```
#!/bin/bash

# Run command 1 and execute command 2 only if it succeeds
command1 && command2

# Run command 1 and execute command 2 only if it fails
command1 || command2
```

3. Error Messages and Logging:

Provide clear and informative error messages when handling errors. Display messages that explain the issue encountered and provide guidance on how to resolve it. Additionally, consider logging errors to a log file for future reference or troubleshooting. For example:

```
#!/bin/bash
```

```
# Run a command and display an error message on failure
if ! command1; then
   echo "Error: Command 1 failed. Please check the configuration."
fi
```

You can redirect error messages to a log file using the 2> redirection operator. For example:

```
#!/bin/bash

# Run a command and log errors to a file
command1 2>/path/to/error.log
```

4. Graceful Exit and Cleanup:

When encountering an error or exception, it's essential to perform proper cleanup tasks before exiting the script. Use the trap command to define cleanup actions or signal handlers. This ensures that resources are released, temporary files are deleted, and any necessary cleanup operations are performed. For example:

```
#!/bin/bash

# Trap a signal and perform cleanup
cleanup() {
  # Cleanup logic
}
```

```
# Set the trap
trap cleanup EXIT

# Script logic
# ...
```

5. Error Codes:

Assign meaningful exit codes to indicate the type of error encountered. By using distinct exit codes, you provide a standardized way for users or other scripts to interpret the script's outcome. Conventionally, an exit code of 0 represents success, while non-zero values indicate different types of errors. Document the error codes in your script or provide a separate document explaining their meanings.

```
#!/bin/bash

# Exit codes
SUCCESS=0
ERROR_INVALID_INPUT=1
ERROR_FILE_NOT_FOUND=2

# Check if a file exists
if [ ! -f "$file" ]; then
  echo "Error: File not found"
  exit $ERROR_FILE_NOT_FOUND
fi
```

By implementing proper error handling techniques, you can create shell scripts that gracefully handle unexpected conditions, provide informative feedback, and ensure the reliability of your code. Taking the time to anticipate and handle errors will enhance the usability and stability of your scripts.

16.3 Code Organization and Modularization

Organizing and modularizing your shell script code is essential for improving readability, maintainability, and reusability. It allows you to break down your script into smaller, manageable components, making it easier to understand and maintain. In this chapter, we will explore strategies for effectively organizing and modularizing your shell script code.

1. Functions:

Functions provide a powerful way to modularize your code by grouping related logic into reusable blocks. Break down complex tasks into smaller, self-contained functions with a clear purpose. This improves code readability and allows you to reuse the same logic in multiple places. For example:

#!/bin/bash

```
# Function to greet a user
greet_user() {
  local name=$1
  echo "Hello, $name!"
}

# Main script
greet_user "John"
```

2. Script Sections:
Divide your script into logical sections, each responsible for a specific task. For example, you can have sections for configuration, input handling, main processing, and output generation. Use comments to clearly mark and describe each section. This helps readers quickly navigate through the script and understand its structure. For example:

```
#!/bin/bash

# Configuration section
# ...

# Input handling section
# ...

# Main processing section
# ...

# Output generation section
# ...
```

3. External Libraries:

Leverage external libraries or utility scripts to handle specific tasks or complex functionalities. This allows you to reuse well-tested code and reduces the amount of code you need to maintain. For example, you can include a utility script for logging, parsing configuration files, or handling common operations. Make sure to document the dependencies and provide instructions for installing or including the required libraries.

```
#!/bin/bash

# Include external library
source "path/to/utility.sh"

# Main script
# ...
```

4. Configuration Files:

Separate configuration settings from your main script by using configuration files. This allows you to modify settings without modifying the script itself, making it easier to manage different environments or scenarios. Store configuration values in a separate file, such as a JSON or INI file, and load them into your script as needed. This promotes flexibility and reusability.

```
#!/bin/bash

# Load configuration from a file
source "path/to/config.json"

# Main script
# ...
```

5. Modular Scripts:

If your script becomes too large or complex, consider splitting it into smaller modular scripts. Each modular script can focus on a specific functionality or task. You can then invoke these scripts from a main script or utilize a master script that orchestrates the execution of the modular scripts. This approach promotes modularity and allows you to manage and test smaller pieces of code independently.

6. Naming Conventions:

Adopt a consistent naming convention for your functions, variables, and files. Use descriptive and meaningful names that convey their purpose. This makes it easier for others to understand your code and promotes consistency across your script. For example, use lowercase with underscores for functions and variables, and choose a clear naming convention for file names.

```
#!/bin/bash
```

```
# Function and variable naming
my_function() {
  local my_variable="value"
}

# File naming
my_script.sh
```

By organizing and modularizing your shell script code, you can improve its readability, maintainability, and reusability. Breaking down your code into smaller, well-defined components makes it easier to understand, update, and collaborate on. With a structured and modular approach, you can create more efficient and robust shell scripts.

16.4 Optimizing Shell Script Performance

Optimizing the performance of your shell scripts is important to ensure efficient execution, reduce resource usage, and improve overall script responsiveness. By following best practices and employing optimization techniques, you can significantly enhance the performance of your shell scripts. In this chapter, we will explore strategies for optimizing shell script performance.

1. Minimize External Commands:

External commands, such as system utilities or complex commands, can introduce overhead and slow down script execution. Whenever possible, try to minimize the use of external commands by utilizing built-in shell functionality and features. Built-in commands execute faster since they don't require launching external processes. Additionally, consider using shell built-in constructs, such as parameter expansion or string manipulation, to perform operations instead of relying on external tools.

2. Use Efficient Loops:

Loops are common in shell scripts, but inefficient loop constructs can degrade script performance. Consider using the most efficient loop construct based on your specific requirements:

- For iterating over a range of numbers, use a for loop instead of a while loop.
- When processing lines from a file, use a while read loop instead of a for loop.
- If possible, leverage tools like awk or sed for efficient text processing instead of looping through each line in a shell script.

3. Optimize File Operations:

File operations can be a performance bottleneck in shell scripts. To optimize file operations, consider the following:

- Minimize the number of file reads and writes by storing frequently accessed data in variables.
- Use file descriptors for efficient file handling instead of repeatedly opening and closing files.
- Use the -exec option or xargs command with find for efficient batch operations on files.

4. Use Shell Options and Optimizations:

Shell options and optimizations can improve script performance. Consider the following:

- Enable shell options like nocaseglob or nullglob to enhance pattern matching performance.
- Set the IFS (Internal Field Separator) variable to a minimal value when processing large amounts of data to reduce unnecessary splitting and parsing.

5. Employ Caching Techniques:

If your script performs repetitive or resource-intensive tasks, consider caching the results to avoid redundant computations. Store computed values in variables or temporary files and reuse them as needed. This reduces the overall execution time and resource consumption.

6. Limit Output and Logging:

Excessive output or logging can impact script performance, especially if it involves writing to disk or network operations. Minimize unnecessary output and logging statements, and consider redirecting output to /dev/null or disabling logging altogether if it's not required.

7. Optimize Data Structures and Algorithms:

Efficient data structures and algorithms can significantly improve script performance. Consider using appropriate data structures, such as arrays or associative arrays, when handling large amounts of data. Additionally, employ efficient algorithms for searching, sorting, or data processing tasks to minimize execution time.

8. Profile and Benchmark:

Profile your script to identify performance bottlenecks and areas for optimization. Use tools like time, strace, or perf to analyze script execution and identify resource-intensive operations. Benchmark different approaches or optimizations to determine their impact on script performance.

By implementing these optimization strategies, you can significantly enhance the performance of your shell scripts. Remember to profile and test your optimizations to ensure they deliver the desired improvements without sacrificing script functionality. With an optimized shell script, you can achieve faster execution times and more efficient resource utilization.

Chapter 17: Automating Tasks with Shell Scripts

Automation is a key benefit of shell scripting, allowing you to save time, streamline repetitive tasks, and increase productivity. In this chapter, we will explore the techniques for automating various tasks using shell scripts.

We will start by understanding the concept of task automation and identifying suitable tasks for automation. You will learn how to analyze your workflow, identify repetitive or time-consuming tasks, and determine the feasibility of automating them with shell scripts.

Next, we will delve into scheduling and executing scripts using tools like cron and at. You will gain insights into scheduling tasks at specific times or intervals, managing script execution, and handling output and error logging.

Furthermore, we will explore file and data processing automation. You will learn how to automate tasks such as file backups, data migrations, log analysis, and report generation. We will cover techniques for traversing directories, manipulating file contents, and performing batch operations on data.

Additionally, we will discuss system administration automation. You will discover how to automate tasks like user management, software installations, system monitoring, and log analysis. You will learn how to leverage shell scripts to streamline these administrative tasks and reduce manual intervention.

Moreover, we will touch upon network automation, including tasks like remote server management, data transfers, and network monitoring. You will gain insights into using tools like SSH and SCP, interacting with APIs, and automating network-related tasks with shell scripts.

By the end of this chapter, you will have a solid understanding of automating tasks with shell scripts. You will be equipped with the skills to identify automation opportunities, schedule and execute scripts, automate file and data processing, streamline system administration tasks, and automate network operations. Get ready to supercharge your productivity by harnessing the power of automation with shell scripts!

17.1 Understanding Automation and Scripting

Automation is the process of automating repetitive tasks or workflows by using technology, tools, or scripts to perform them automatically. Automation can save time, increase efficiency, reduce errors, and allow for consistent and reliable execution of tasks. Scripting, specifically shell scripting, is a powerful method for automating tasks on Unix-like systems. In this chapter, we will explore the concepts and benefits of automation and scripting.

1. What is Automation?

Automation involves replacing manual, repetitive tasks with automated processes that can be executed by machines. It allows you to streamline workflows, reduce human effort, and improve productivity. Automation can be applied to various domains, including system administration, software deployment, data processing, file management, and more.

2. Why Use Shell Scripting for Automation?

Shell scripting, particularly with Bash, is a popular choice for automation on Unix-like systems. Here are some reasons why:

- **Accessibility**: Shell scripting is widely available on Unix-like systems, making it accessible to users across various platforms.
- **Versatility**: Shell scripting provides access to a wide range of system utilities and commands, allowing for flexible and powerful automation capabilities.

- **Integration**: Shell scripts can interact with other system components, such as files, processes, and networks, making it easy to integrate automation with existing infrastructure.
- **Customization**: Shell scripts can be tailored to specific needs and requirements, allowing for the creation of customized automation solutions.

Portability: Shell scripts can be easily shared and executed on different Unix-like systems without the need for major modifications.

3. Benefits of Automation and Scripting:

Automation and scripting offer several benefits, including:

- **Time Savings**: By automating repetitive tasks, you can save significant amounts of time and focus on more critical or creative work.
- **Increased Efficiency**: Automation eliminates manual errors and ensures consistent and reliable execution of tasks.
- **Consistency**: Automation enforces standardized processes and eliminates variations that can arise from manual execution.

- **Scalability**: Automated scripts can handle large volumes of work and scale easily as the workload increases.
- **Enhanced Productivity**: Automation frees up human resources to focus on higher-value activities, leading to increased productivity.
- **Error Reduction**: Automation reduces the risk of human errors that can occur during manual execution of tasks.
- **Rapid Deployment**: With automation, tasks can be executed quickly and repeatedly, allowing for rapid deployment of processes or changes.
- **Auditing and Tracking**: Automation provides an audit trail and tracking of executed tasks, aiding in troubleshooting and compliance.

4. Use Cases for Automation and Scripting:

Automation and scripting find applications in various domains, including:

- **System Administration**: Automating system configuration, software installation, user management, backups, and monitoring tasks.
- **DevOps**: Automating software builds, deployments, testing, and continuous integration/continuous deployment (CI/CD) pipelines.
- **Data Processing**: Automating data ingestion, transformation, validation, and reporting tasks.

- **File Management**: Automating file operations, such as renaming, copying, moving, or archiving files.
- **Task Scheduling**: Automating the execution of tasks at predefined intervals or based on specific events.
- **Network Management**: Automating network configurations, monitoring, and troubleshooting tasks.
- **Security and Compliance**: Automating security scans, vulnerability assessments, and compliance checks.

Automation and scripting empower users to achieve greater efficiency, consistency, and reliability in their workflows. By leveraging the power of shell scripting, you can automate a wide range of tasks and processes, freeing up valuable time and resources for more strategic activities.

17.2 Creating Simple Automation Scripts

Automation scripts are powerful tools for streamlining repetitive tasks and improving efficiency in various domains. By writing simple automation scripts, you can automate routine processes and save valuable time and effort. In this chapter, we will explore the process of creating simple automation scripts using shell scripting.

1. Identify the Task to Automate:

Begin by identifying the specific task or process you want to automate. It can be a repetitive task, a series of commands, or a sequence of operations that you perform regularly. Clearly define the inputs, outputs, and desired outcome of the task.

2. Plan the Script:

Once you have identified the task, plan the steps required to automate it. Break down the task into smaller subtasks or commands that need to be executed in a specific order. Determine the logic and decision-making process, if applicable.

3. Choose the Scripting Language:

In this case, you will be using shell scripting, specifically Bash, for automation. Ensure that Bash is available on your system. If not, install it. Bash provides a wide range of built-in commands and utilities that can be utilized in your automation scripts.

4. Create a New Script File:

Open a text editor and create a new file with a .sh extension. This extension indicates that it is a shell script. For example, you can use the command nano script.sh to create a new file named "script.sh".

5. Set the Script Header:

Begin the script by adding a shebang line, which specifies the interpreter to be used. For Bash scripts, the shebang line should be #!/bin/bash. This ensures that the script is executed by the Bash interpreter.

6. Write the Script Code:

Based on your planned steps from Step 2, start writing the script code. Use Bash's syntax and built-in commands to implement the required functionality. You can perform various operations, such as file manipulation, command execution, conditional statements, loops, and more.

7. Test and Debug the Script:

After writing the script code, save the file and make it executable using the chmod +x script.sh command. To test the script, execute it by running ./script.sh in the terminal. Verify that it produces the desired results and behaves as expected. If any issues arise, debug the script by using echo statements or by checking for error messages.

8. Refine and Enhance the Script:

Once the script is functioning correctly, consider refining and enhancing it further. Look for opportunities to optimize the script code, improve error handling, add logging or notifications, or incorporate additional functionality as needed.

9. Document and Maintain the Script:

Document the purpose, usage, and any specific instructions related to the script. This will help you and others understand and utilize the script effectively. Maintain the script by reviewing and updating it periodically to accommodate any changes in the task or underlying system.

By following these steps, you can create simple automation scripts using shell scripting. Start with small, manageable tasks and gradually expand your scripting skills to tackle more complex automation scenarios. Automation scripts can save you time, increase productivity, and improve the consistency and reliability of your workflow.

17.3 Scheduling Scripts with cron

Scheduling scripts to run automatically at predefined intervals is a crucial aspect of automation. The cron utility, available in Unix-like systems, provides a convenient way to schedule and execute scripts or commands at specific times or intervals. In this chapter, we will explore the usage of cron for scheduling and automating tasks.

1. Understanding cron:

cron is a time-based job scheduler in Unix-like operating systems. It allows users to schedule the execution of scripts or commands at specific times, dates, or intervals. The cron utility uses a configuration file called crontab (cron table) to define the scheduled tasks.

2. Accessing the crontab:

To access the crontab for a user, you can use the command crontab -e. This opens the crontab file in the default editor. Each user has their own crontab file, allowing them to define their own scheduled tasks independently.

3. Editing the crontab:

The crontab file consists of individual lines, each representing a scheduled task. Each line follows a specific format that specifies the schedule and the command or script to execute. The general syntax of a cron schedule entry is as follows:

* * * * * command_to_be_executed

The five asterisks (*) represent the time and date fields for minute, hour, day of the month, month, and day of the week, respectively. You can set specific values or use wildcard characters to represent all possible values.

4. Specifying the schedule:

To define the schedule, you need to specify the desired values in the respective time and date fields. For example, to run a script every day at 2:30 PM, you can use the following crontab entry:

30 14 * * * /path/to/script.sh

The values 30 and 14 represent the minute and hour fields, respectively, followed by the wildcard (*) for the day of the month, month, and day of the week fields. The /path/to/script.sh represents the absolute path to the script that needs to be executed.

5. Additional scheduling options:

In addition to specifying exact time and date values, cron provides a set of special characters that allow for more flexible scheduling:

- **Asterisk (*):** Represents all possible values in a field.

- **Comma (,):** Specifies multiple values. For example, 1,5,10 represents the 1st, 5th, and 10th of the month.
- **Hyphen (-):** Defines a range of values. For example, 1-5 represents the 1st to 5th of the month.
- **Forward slash (/):** Indicates a step value. For example, */5 represents every 5 units (e.g., every 5 minutes).

6. Redirecting output:

By default, cron sends the output of scheduled tasks to the user's email. To redirect the output to a file, you can modify the crontab entry as follows:

30 14 * * * /path/to/script.sh > /path/to/output.log 2>&1

The > /path/to/output.log redirects the standard output to the specified file, while 2>&1 redirects the standard error to the same file.

7. Verifying and managing cron jobs:

To list the existing cron jobs, you can use the command crontab -l. This displays the scheduled tasks defined in the crontab. If you want to remove all scheduled tasks, you can run crontab -r. To edit an existing crontab, use crontab -e again.

8. System-wide cron jobs:

In addition to user-specific crontab files, Unix-like systems also provide system-wide crontab files located in /etc/crontab or /etc/cron.d. These files allow system administrators to define tasks that run with root privileges.

Scheduling scripts with cron offers a powerful means of automating tasks on Unix-like systems. By utilizing the flexibility and precision of cron scheduling, you can ensure that your scripts or commands run automatically at the desired intervals, freeing you from manual execution and increasing overall efficiency.

17.4 Using Shell Scripts in Workflow Automation

Shell scripts are powerful tools for automating workflows and streamlining repetitive tasks. In this chapter, we will explore how shell scripts can be integrated into workflow automation to enhance productivity and efficiency.

1. Identifying Workflow Automation Opportunities:

The first step in using shell scripts for workflow automation is to identify the tasks or processes that can benefit from automation. Look for repetitive or time-consuming tasks that can be easily automated using a script. This could include tasks such as data processing, file management, system administration, and more.

2. Designing the Workflow:

Once you have identified the tasks to automate, design the workflow by breaking it down into smaller steps. Determine the logical sequence of these steps and consider any dependencies or conditions that need to be satisfied for successful automation. This will help in structuring your shell script accordingly.

3. Creating the Shell Script:

With the workflow defined, start creating the shell script that will automate the tasks. Begin by writing the necessary commands and logic to perform each step of the workflow. Utilize the concepts and techniques covered in earlier chapters, such as conditional statements, loops, file operations, and string manipulation, to build a robust and efficient script.

4. Input and Output Handling:

Consider how the script will interact with the user or other components of the workflow. Determine if any input parameters need to be provided when executing the script and incorporate mechanisms to handle user prompts or input files. Similarly, ensure that the script generates appropriate output or logs to track the progress and results of the automated workflow.

5. Error Handling and Logging:

Implement error handling mechanisms within the script to handle unexpected situations or errors that may occur during automation. Use conditional statements, try-catch blocks, or other error handling techniques to gracefully handle exceptions and provide meaningful error messages. Additionally, implement logging mechanisms to capture important information, errors, or debugging details for future reference.

6. Integration with Other Tools and Systems:

Consider how the shell script will integrate with other tools or systems in your workflow. This may involve invoking external commands, interacting with APIs, accessing databases, or communicating with other scripts or services. Ensure that the necessary interfaces and integration points are properly implemented in your script.

7. Testing and Iteration:

Thoroughly test your shell script to ensure it functions as expected and produces the desired results. Test different scenarios and edge cases to validate the robustness of the automation. Make necessary iterations and improvements based on the testing results to enhance the script's reliability and performance.

8. Documentation and Maintenance:

Document the purpose, usage, and functionality of the shell script to facilitate future maintenance and collaboration. Include instructions on how to execute the script, any required dependencies, and potential configuration options. Regularly review and maintain the script to accommodate changes in the workflow or underlying systems.

By effectively using shell scripts in workflow automation, you can save time, reduce errors, and increase productivity in your day-to-day tasks. The flexibility and versatility of shell scripting make it an invaluable tool for automating various processes, enabling you to focus on more critical aspects of your work.

Chapter 18: Introduction to Shell Scripting Tools and Utilities

In this chapter, we will explore various tools and utilities that can enhance your shell scripting experience. These tools offer additional functionality, simplify common tasks, and provide solutions to specific scripting challenges.

We will start by introducing text processing tools such as awk, sed, and grep. You will learn how these powerful utilities can be used to manipulate and analyze text data, perform pattern matching, extract specific information, and transform text in various ways.

Next, we will dive into the world of version control systems, specifically Git. You will discover how Git can be integrated into your shell scripts, enabling you to automate tasks such as code versioning, branching, merging, and deployment.

Furthermore, we will explore scripting frameworks and libraries that extend the capabilities of shell scripting. You will learn about popular frameworks like Bash-it and libraries like ShellCheck, which provide additional features, code linting, and error checking for your shell scripts.

Additionally, we will discuss debugging and profiling tools for shell scripts. You will gain insights into utilities such as shellcheck, bashdb, and shell-prof, which help you identify and resolve errors, optimize script performance, and gain a deeper understanding of script execution.

Moreover, we will touch upon scripting documentation generators like Markdown and tools such as Pandoc that allow you to generate professional-looking documentation from your shell scripts.

By exploring these tools and utilities, you will have a broader toolkit to enhance your shell scripting capabilities. Whether it's text processing, version control, debugging, or documentation, these tools will empower you to write more efficient, maintainable, and professional shell scripts. Get ready to explore the vast ecosystem of shell scripting tools and utilities and take your scripting skills to the next level!

18.1 Introduction to External Commands and Utilities

In addition to the built-in commands and capabilities of the shell, shell scripting allows you to leverage a wide range of external commands and utilities to enhance the functionality of your scripts. These external tools provide specialized features and functionality that can be seamlessly integrated into your shell scripts.

1. What are External Commands and Utilities?

External commands and utilities are standalone programs or scripts that are separate from the shell itself. They are typically developed to perform specific tasks or provide additional functionality beyond what the shell offers. These tools are often written in languages like C, Python, Perl, or Ruby and are designed to be executed from the command line.

2. Common Examples of External Commands and Utilities:

There is a vast ecosystem of external commands and utilities available for various purposes. Some commonly used examples include:

- **grep**: A powerful tool for searching and filtering text using regular expressions.
- **sed**: A stream editor for manipulating text streams using regular expressions and various commands.
- **awk**: A versatile programming language for processing and analyzing text files.
- **curl**: A command-line tool for making HTTP requests and transferring data using various protocols.

- **tar**: A utility for creating and manipulating archive files.
- **rsync**: A fast and versatile file synchronization and transfer tool.
- **ssh**: A secure shell protocol for securely accessing remote systems.
- **find**: A tool for searching and locating files based on various criteria.
- **sort**: A command for sorting lines of text in a file or from standard input.
- **cut**: A tool for extracting specific sections (columns) of text from files or input streams.

These are just a few examples, and there are numerous other external commands and utilities available that can greatly expand the capabilities of your shell scripts.

3. Incorporating External Commands into Shell Scripts:

To use external commands within your shell scripts, you can simply invoke them by their name and provide any required arguments or options. The shell will spawn a separate process to execute the command, and the output (if any) can be captured or processed as needed.

For example, to use the grep command within a shell script to search for a specific pattern in a file, you can write:

```
grep "pattern" file.txt
```

Similarly, you can assign the output of an external command to a variable or use it as input for further processing within your script.

4. Exploring Command Documentation:

When working with external commands and utilities, it is essential to refer to their documentation or manual pages to understand their usage, available options, and syntax. Most commands have detailed documentation accessible through the man command, providing comprehensive information on their functionality and usage examples.

5. Installing Additional Commands and Utilities:

While many external commands come pre-installed with the operating system, some may need to be installed separately. Package managers like apt, yum, or brew can be used to install additional tools based on the specific operating system or distribution you are using. Ensure that you have the necessary permissions and follow the installation instructions provided for each command or utility.

By leveraging external commands and utilities, you can extend the capabilities of your shell scripts and achieve more complex and specialized tasks.

Whether it's text processing, network operations, file management, or system administration, the rich ecosystem of external tools opens up a world of possibilities for automating and enhancing your shell scripts.

18.2 Using Standard Unix Utilities in Scripts

Standard Unix utilities provide a set of powerful tools that can be effectively utilized within your shell scripts. These utilities offer various functionalities for text processing, file manipulation, system administration, and more. In this chapter, we will explore how to incorporate some commonly used standard Unix utilities into your scripts.

1. grep:

The grep utility is widely used for searching and filtering text based on patterns. You can use it to search for specific strings or patterns in files or input streams. Incorporating grep into your script allows you to extract relevant information or filter data based on specific criteria.

2. sed:

sed (stream editor) is a versatile tool for performing text transformations. It allows you to perform tasks such as substitution, deletion, insertion, and more on lines of text. By integrating sed into your script, you can manipulate and modify text files or streams according to your requirements.

3. awk:

awk is a powerful programming language designed for text processing and data extraction. It provides rich capabilities for parsing, filtering, and manipulating structured text data. With awk, you can perform complex operations on fields, apply conditional actions, and generate reports. By incorporating awk into your script, you can process and extract meaningful information from text data.

4. cut:

The cut command allows you to extract specific fields or columns from lines of text. It is particularly useful for parsing structured data where fields are delimited by a specific character. You can use cut to isolate relevant fields from files or input streams within your script.

5. sort:

The sort command provides functionality for sorting lines of text. It allows you to sort data alphabetically, numerically, in reverse order, and based on various criteria. Integrating sort into your script enables you to organize and arrange data in a desired order.

6. tr:

The tr command is used for translating or deleting characters in a text stream. It can perform tasks such as character substitution, character deletion, and character squeezing. By utilizing tr in your script, you can transform and manipulate text data according to your needs.

7. find:

The find command is a powerful tool for searching and locating files and directories based on specified criteria. It supports various search parameters, including file name patterns, size, modification time, and more. By incorporating find into your script, you can automate file searches and perform operations on the discovered files.

8. xargs:

The xargs command allows you to build and execute commands based on input from standard input or files. It is particularly useful when you need to process a large number of files or provide input to another command. Integrating xargs into your script enables you to efficiently handle complex command pipelines or iterate over files.

These are just a few examples of standard Unix utilities that can be incorporated into your shell scripts. By leveraging the functionality provided by these tools, you can enhance the capabilities of your scripts and accomplish a wide range of tasks efficiently and effectively. Refer to the respective utility's documentation or manual pages for detailed usage information and explore additional options and features they offer.

18.3 Commonly Used Shell Scripting Tools and Libraries

When writing shell scripts, you can make use of various tools and libraries that provide additional functionalities, simplify common tasks, and enhance the overall scripting experience. In this chapter, we will explore some commonly used shell scripting tools and libraries that can significantly aid in your script development process.

1. ShellCheck:

ShellCheck is a static analysis tool for shell scripts that helps identify common errors, inconsistencies, and best practice violations. It scans your script and provides suggestions to improve its quality and reliability. ShellCheck can be integrated into your development workflow to catch potential issues early and ensure adherence to good scripting practices.

2. jq:

jq is a lightweight and flexible command-line tool for processing and manipulating JSON data. It provides a convenient way to extract, filter, and transform JSON structures, making it invaluable when working with APIs or handling JSON-based configurations in your scripts. jq's simple and expressive syntax enables you to perform complex operations on JSON data effortlessly.

3. dialog:

The dialog utility allows you to create text-based dialog boxes and interactive menus within your shell scripts. It provides a way to present information, prompts, and options to users in a user-friendly manner. By incorporating dialog into your scripts, you can create interactive interfaces, gather user input, and facilitate decision-making processes.

4. expect:

The expect utility enables scripted interaction with other command-line applications that require user input or respond to prompts. It automates interactive sessions, allowing you to script actions such as providing passwords, answering questions, or handling various prompts. expect is particularly useful when automating interactions with programs that do not have built-in automation capabilities.

5. curl:

curl is a versatile command-line tool for making HTTP requests and interacting with various network protocols. It supports a wide range of features, including sending GET and POST requests, handling authentication, handling cookies, and more. curl can be integrated into your shell scripts to interact with web services, download files, or perform other network-related operations.

6. parallel:

parallel is a powerful command-line tool that enables parallel execution of shell commands or scripts. It allows you to distribute tasks across multiple CPU cores, significantly improving script execution times for computationally intensive or parallelizable tasks. parallel provides a straightforward way to harness the full potential of your system's resources.

7. getopt:

The getopt utility simplifies the handling of command-line options and arguments in your shell scripts. It provides a standardized way to parse command-line options, validate their presence, and extract their values. getopt helps you build robust and user-friendly scripts with proper option handling and usage information.

8. GNU Core Utilities:

The GNU Core Utilities, commonly available on Unix-like systems, provide a comprehensive set of essential command-line tools. These utilities include tools like cat, grep, sed, awk, cut, and more. Leveraging these utilities can save you time and effort by allowing you to rely on widely tested and optimized implementations of common tasks.

9. Shell Script Libraries:

Various shell script libraries are available that offer additional functions and utilities for specific tasks. For example, the Bash Infinity library provides advanced functions for error handling, logging, testing, and more. Similarly, the Bash Automated Testing System (BATS) library helps in writing automated tests for your scripts. Exploring and utilizing such libraries can greatly enhance the functionality and maintainability of your shell scripts.

These are just a few examples of commonly used shell scripting tools and libraries. Depending on your specific requirements, you may come across additional tools or libraries that suit your needs. Always refer to the respective documentation and resources for detailed usage instructions and explore how these tools can streamline your scripting process and make your scripts more robust and efficient.

Chapter 19: Interacting with the Operating System

In this chapter, we will delve into the techniques for interacting with the operating system from within your shell scripts. Understanding how to interact with the underlying OS allows you to access system information, execute system commands, and perform advanced system-related tasks.

We will start by exploring commands and utilities that provide information about the system. You will learn how to retrieve system details such as the hostname, current user, system architecture, kernel version, and available hardware resources. This knowledge will enable you to adapt your scripts based on the system environment.

Next, we will dive into executing system commands from within your scripts. You will discover how to run system commands using functions like system(), exec(), or backticks, and capture their output for further processing. We will also cover techniques for handling command output, error handling, and managing command execution.

Furthermore, we will discuss techniques for system monitoring and performance analysis. You will learn how to retrieve system metrics such as CPU usage, memory usage, disk space, and network statistics.

We will explore tools and utilities that provide insights into system performance and demonstrate how to integrate them into your scripts.

Additionally, we will touch upon system configuration and customization. You will gain insights into modifying system settings, managing system services, and working with configuration files. You will learn how to automate system configuration tasks, ensuring consistency and efficiency.

Moreover, we will explore system security considerations. You will learn techniques for user management, access control, and securing sensitive data within your scripts. We will discuss best practices for handling passwords, securely transferring data, and implementing secure communication protocols.

By the end of this chapter, you will have a solid understanding of interacting with the operating system from your shell scripts. You will be equipped with the skills to retrieve system information, execute system commands, monitor system performance, and customize system configuration. Get ready to leverage the power of your operating system and unleash the full potential of your shell scripts!

19.1 Gathering System Information

When writing shell scripts, it's often useful to gather information about the system on which the script is running. This information can help you make informed decisions, perform system-specific tasks, or provide diagnostic details. In this chapter, we will explore various ways to gather system information using shell scripting.

1. uname:

The uname command provides basic information about the system, such as the kernel name, hostname, operating system, and architecture. You can use the output of uname within your script to determine the system type and adjust the script behavior accordingly.

2. hostname:

The hostname command retrieves the hostname of the system. It can be useful for identifying the system or generating dynamic output based on the hostname.

3. date:

The date command displays the current date and time. You can use it to include timestamps in log files or generate time-based filenames.

4. uptime:

The uptime command provides information about the system's uptime, load average, and number of logged-in users. This can be valuable for monitoring system performance or determining system availability.

5. df:

The df command displays information about available disk space on file systems. It can help you track disk usage, identify potential space constraints, or generate reports.

6. free:

The free command shows information about system memory usage, including total, used, and available memory. It can be helpful for monitoring memory usage or diagnosing memory-related issues.

7. ifconfig/ip:

The ifconfig command (or ip command on newer systems) provides network interface configuration information. It can retrieve details such as IP addresses, network masks, and interface status. This information is particularly useful for network-related tasks or troubleshooting.

8. lspci/lsusb:

The lspci command lists information about PCI devices connected to the system, while lsusb lists information about USB devices. You can use these commands to identify hardware components, retrieve device IDs, or check for driver compatibility.

9. sysctl:

The sysctl command allows you to retrieve and modify kernel parameters and system settings. It can be used to gather information about various aspects of the system's configuration or adjust specific settings.

10. proc file system:

The /proc file system in Linux provides a wealth of system information. You can access information about processes, system statistics, hardware, and more by reading files under the /proc directory. This allows you to gather detailed system information programmatically.

By utilizing these commands and techniques within your shell scripts, you can gather valuable system information and utilize it for various purposes. Whether it's customizing script behavior based on system type, monitoring system performance, or troubleshooting issues, understanding and utilizing system information is crucial for effective shell scripting.

19.2 Managing Users and Groups

Shell scripting provides powerful tools for managing users and groups on a Unix-like system. In this chapter, we will explore various commands and techniques that can be used to create, modify, and delete users and groups programmatically.

1. useradd/userdel:

The useradd command is used to create new user accounts, while userdel is used to delete existing user accounts. These commands allow you to specify various options such as the user's home directory, default shell, user ID, and group membership.

2. usermod:

The usermod command enables you to modify user account properties, such as the username, home directory, default shell, or group membership. It provides flexibility in managing user details without having to delete and recreate the user account.

3. groupadd/groupdel:

The groupadd command is used to create new groups, while groupdel is used to delete existing groups. You can specify options such as the group ID and initial group members when creating a group.

4. groupmod:

The groupmod command allows you to modify group properties, such as the group name or group ID. You can also add or remove users from a group using the groupmod command.

5. passwd:

The passwd command is used to set or change the password for a user account. It can be used in shell scripts to automate password management for newly created user accounts or to enforce password changes.

6. chown/chgrp:

The chown command changes the ownership of files and directories, while chgrp changes the group ownership. These commands are useful for granting ownership to specific users or groups or for ensuring proper file permissions within a script.

7. id:

The id command displays information about a user or group, including the user ID (UID), group ID (GID), and group memberships. It can be used to retrieve user or group information within a script.

8. getent:

The getent command retrieves information from various system databases, including user and group databases. It can be used to programmatically obtain user or group details, such as the user's home directory or the group members.

9. /etc/passwd and /etc/group:

The /etc/passwd file stores user account information, including usernames, user IDs, home directories, and default shells. The /etc/group file contains group information, including group names, group IDs, and group members. You can read and manipulate these files within your shell scripts to perform user and group management tasks.

By utilizing these commands and techniques, you can automate user and group management tasks, ensure consistent configurations across systems, and streamline administrative processes. However, it's important to exercise caution and follow security best practices when writing scripts that involve user and group management to avoid unintended consequences or security vulnerabilities.

19.3 Interacting with Services and Daemons

In a Unix-like system, services and daemons are crucial components that provide various functionalities. As a shell script developer, you may need to interact with these services and daemons programmatically. In this chapter, we will explore different ways to interact with services and daemons using shell scripting.

1. service/systemctl:

The service command (or systemctl on systemd-based systems) is used to start, stop, restart, or reload services. It allows you to control the execution of system services and manage their behavior. You can use these commands in your shell scripts to automate service management tasks.

2. init.d scripts/systemd unit files:

System services are typically controlled through init scripts or systemd unit files. Init scripts are located in the /etc/init.d directory, while systemd unit files are stored in various directories such as /etc/systemd/system. You can invoke these scripts or unit files directly from your shell scripts to interact with services and daemons.

3. kill:

The kill command is used to send signals to processes, allowing you to control their behavior. By specifying the process ID (PID) or process name, you can send signals such as SIGTERM or SIGKILL to start or stop processes. This can be useful for managing long-running daemons or controlling background processes.

4. ps:

The ps command provides information about currently running processes. You can use it to retrieve the process ID (PID) or other details of specific processes. By combining ps with other commands or tools, you can perform tasks such as checking if a particular daemon is running or monitoring process status.

5. netstat/ss:

The netstat command (or ss command on newer systems) displays network-related information, including open ports and active network connections. It can be used to check if a service is listening on a specific port or to identify network-related issues. Incorporating netstat or ss output into your scripts can help you interact with services based on their network availability.

6. log files:

Many services and daemons write log files to record their activities and capture important information. You can read and parse these log files within your shell scripts to extract specific details or perform troubleshooting tasks. By interacting with log files, you can gain insights into the behavior of services and daemons.

7. configuration files:

Services and daemons often have configuration files that control their settings and behavior. You can programmatically modify these configuration files using text processing tools like sed or awk within your shell scripts. This allows you to automate configuration changes or ensure consistent configurations across systems.

By leveraging these methods to interact with services and daemons, you can automate the management and monitoring of critical system components. This enables you to streamline administrative tasks, ensure service availability, and troubleshoot issues efficiently using shell scripting.

19.4 File System Operations and Permissions

When working with shell scripting, it is essential to understand file system operations and permissions. In this chapter, we will explore various techniques for manipulating files and directories, as well as managing permissions within a Unix-like system.

1. File Operations:

- **Creating Files and Directories**: Shell scripting allows you to create new files and directories using commands such as touch and mkdir. These commands can be used to automate the creation of necessary file structures.
- **Copying and Moving Files**: You can use commands like cp and mv to copy or move files and directories within your shell scripts. This is useful for automating backup processes or organizing files.
- **Deleting Files and Directories**: The rm command is used to remove files and directories. Within a shell script, you can utilize this command to delete unwanted files or clean up directories.

2. File Permissions:

- **Changing File Permissions**: The chmod command enables you to modify file permissions. By specifying the desired permission settings, you can grant or revoke read, write, and execute permissions for users, groups, and others.
- **Viewing File Permissions**: The ls command with the -l option displays detailed information about files, including their permissions. You can use this command within your scripts to retrieve and analyze file permissions programmatically.

3. File Ownership:

- **Changing File Ownership**: The chown command allows you to change the ownership of files and directories. Within a shell script, you can assign ownership to specific users or groups programmatically.
- **Viewing File Ownership**: The ls command with the -l option also displays the owner and group information for files. You can incorporate this command into your scripts to retrieve owner and group details.

4. File Permissions Mask:

Understanding the umask: The umask is a permission mask that determines the default permissions for newly created files and directories. Within your scripts, you can modify the umask value using the umask command to ensure specific default permissions.

5. Symbolic and Numeric Permissions:

- **Symbolic Permissions**: Symbolic permissions represent file permissions using symbols like r (read), w (write), and x (execute). By combining these symbols with the user, group, and others' indicators, you can set or modify permissions programmatically.
- **Numeric Permissions**: Numeric permissions use octal representation (e.g., 755, 644) to specify file permissions. You can assign these values using the chmod command within your scripts.

Understanding file system operations and permissions is crucial for effective shell scripting. It allows you to automate file-related tasks, control access to files and directories, and ensure data security and integrity within your system.

Chapter 20: Writing Portable Shell Scripts

Writing portable shell scripts ensures that your scripts can run consistently across different operating systems, shell environments, and versions. In this chapter, we will explore the techniques and best practices for writing portable shell scripts that can be executed reliably on various platforms.

We will start by discussing the importance of understanding shell compatibility. You will learn about different shell environments such as Bash, POSIX-compliant shells, and other popular shells. Understanding the limitations and differences between these shells will enable you to write scripts that are compatible across a wide range of systems.

Next, we will explore portable scripting constructs and practices. You will learn how to use POSIX-compliant syntax, avoid shell-specific features, and adhere to common scripting conventions. We will cover topics such as variable declaration, command substitution, loops, and conditional statements in a portable manner.

Furthermore, we will discuss handling common pitfalls and challenges when writing portable scripts. You will gain insights into dealing with differences in command-line arguments, file paths, environment variables, and command output across different platforms. We will explore techniques for detecting and working around these platform-specific differences.

Additionally, we will touch upon portability testing and validation. You will learn how to test your scripts on different systems and shell environments, using tools like virtual machines or containers. We will discuss techniques for identifying and resolving compatibility issues to ensure your scripts run seamlessly across diverse environments.

Moreover, we will explore the concept of wrapper scripts and platform-specific configuration files. You will discover how to create wrapper scripts that adapt your script's behavior based on the underlying system. We will also discuss strategies for handling platform-specific configurations through external files or environment variables.

By following the principles and techniques presented in this chapter, you will be able to write portable shell scripts that can be executed consistently across different platforms. Your scripts will be versatile, adaptable, and compatible, allowing users to run them in various environments without modification. Get ready to embrace portability and create robust shell scripts that transcend system boundaries!

20.1 Understanding Shell Script Portability

When writing shell scripts, it is essential to consider their portability across different Unix-like systems. Shell script portability refers to the ability of a script to run consistently and correctly across various operating systems, shells, and environments. In this chapter, we will explore the concept of shell script portability and techniques for writing portable shell scripts.

1. Choosing a Shell:

Different Unix-like systems may use different default shells, such as Bash, Zsh, or Dash. To ensure portability, it is recommended to use POSIX-compliant shell syntax, which is supported by most shells. This allows your scripts to run on a wide range of systems without relying on shell-specific features.

2. Avoiding Bash-Dependent Features:

Bash, being a powerful shell with extended features, offers capabilities beyond the POSIX standard. While these features can be advantageous, using them in your scripts can limit their portability. It is best to stick to POSIX-compliant syntax and avoid Bash-specific features, unless you specifically target Bash as the required shell.

3. Using Portable Command Options and Flags:

Commands often have different options and flags across different systems. To ensure portability, use command options and flags that are common and supported across various platforms. Be cautious when relying on specific behavior or options that might not be available on all systems.

4. Handling Command and Utility Variations:

Commands and utilities may have slight variations in their behavior, command-line options, or output format across different systems. To write portable scripts, account for these variations by using conditional statements or checking for the presence of specific commands or utilities before invoking them.

5. Using Portable Pathnames:

File and directory pathnames can differ across systems, particularly in terms of the directory structure and separator characters. To write portable scripts, avoid hardcoding absolute paths and instead use relative paths or environment variables such as $HOME or $PATH.

6. Considering System-Specific Configurations:

Different systems may have their own configuration files, environment variables, or default settings. When writing portable scripts, take into account these system-specific configurations and adapt your scripts accordingly. Make use of environment variables or command-line arguments to allow users to customize the script's behavior based on their system's configuration.

7. Testing and Validating on Different Systems:

To ensure the portability of your shell scripts, it is crucial to test and validate them on different target systems. Set up test environments with various operating systems and shell versions to identify any compatibility issues and make necessary adjustments.

By following these guidelines and writing portable shell scripts, you can ensure that your scripts can be executed reliably on different Unix-like systems. This allows your scripts to be more widely applicable, reusable, and accessible to users across various environments.

20.2 Writing POSIX-Compliant Shell Scripts

Writing POSIX-compliant shell scripts ensures maximum portability across different Unix-like systems. POSIX (Portable Operating System Interface) is a set of standards that define a common interface for Unix-like operating systems. Adhering to POSIX standards allows your shell scripts to run consistently and reliably on various platforms. In this chapter, we will explore techniques for writing POSIX-compliant shell scripts.

1. Shell Selection:

Choose a POSIX-compliant shell as the interpreter for your script. Common options include sh, bash, and dash. Avoid using shell-specific features that may not be supported by all POSIX-compliant shells.

2. Use Portable Syntax:

Stick to the core POSIX shell syntax, which is supported by most shells. Avoid using non-standard or shell-specific syntax elements, as they may not be available in all environments.

3. Avoid Bash-Dependent Features:

While Bash offers powerful features beyond the POSIX standard, relying on them limits the portability of your script. Avoid using Bash-specific syntax, options, or built-in functions unless targeting a system where Bash is explicitly required.

4. Portable Command Execution:

Ensure that the commands and utilities used in your script are POSIX-compliant and available on most systems. Avoid using system-specific or non-standard commands. Check for the existence of commands before using them or provide alternative approaches when necessary.

5. Handling Command Options and Flags:

Use command options and flags that are commonly supported across different platforms. Be cautious when relying on specific behavior or options that might not be available on all systems. Consider using portable alternatives or conditional statements to handle command variations.

6. Pathname Considerations:

Be mindful of pathname differences across systems, such as directory structure and separator characters. Avoid hardcoding absolute paths and instead use relative paths or environment variables like $HOME or $PATH to ensure portability.

7. Standard Input and Output:

Use the standard input and output mechanisms provided by POSIX shells. Avoid relying on non-standard redirections or I/O operations that may not be universally supported.

8. Environment Variables:

Prefer using standard environment variables defined by POSIX, such as $HOME or $PATH. Avoid relying on system-specific environment variables, as they may vary across platforms.

9. Error Handling:

Follow POSIX conventions for error handling. Use exit codes and standard error output (stderr) for reporting errors. Avoid relying on shell-specific error handling mechanisms.

10. Testing and Validation:

Validate your script on different POSIX-compliant systems to ensure its portability. Test on various Unix-like platforms with different shell versions to identify and resolve compatibility issues.

By adhering to POSIX standards and avoiding shell-specific features, you can write shell scripts that are highly portable and compatible with a wide range of Unix-like systems. POSIX-compliant scripts are more likely to run reliably and consistently, ensuring broad accessibility and usability across diverse environments.

20.3 Dealing with Platform-Specific Differences

When writing shell scripts, it's important to consider platform-specific differences that may exist across different Unix-like systems. While aiming for portability is ideal, there are cases where you may need to handle platform-specific variations. In this chapter, we will explore techniques for dealing with platform-specific differences in your shell scripts.

1. Conditional Statements:

Use conditional statements to check for specific platform features or behaviors. By detecting the underlying platform or shell version, you can adapt your script accordingly. For example, you can use uname or other system-specific commands to determine the operating system and apply platform-specific logic.

2. Command Availability:

Check for the availability of commands or utilities before using them. Use conditional statements or the command or which commands to verify if a particular command is present on the system. This allows you to provide fallback options or alternative approaches for systems where the command is missing or behaves differently.

3. Command Options and Flags:

Different versions of commands may have varying options or flags. To handle platform-specific differences, use conditional statements or command-specific checks to determine the appropriate options or flags based on the underlying platform.

4. Filesystem Variations:

Filesystem structures and conventions may differ across platforms. When dealing with files and directories, consider using platform-independent path handling techniques, such as the dirname and basename commands or the readlink utility. Avoid assuming specific filesystem layouts or relying on non-standard features.

5. Environment Variables:

Be aware of platform-specific environment variables that may differ across systems. Instead, rely on standard environment variables defined by POSIX or use command-line arguments to pass necessary information to your script. This ensures consistent behavior regardless of platform.

6. Utility and Command Compatibility:

Some commands and utilities may have variations in behavior or options between platforms. It is essential to thoroughly test your script on different systems and versions to ensure compatibility. Consider using the least common denominator of command features to maximize portability.

7. Documentation and User Instructions:

Clearly document any platform-specific requirements or variations in your script's documentation or user instructions. Provide guidance on how to handle platform-specific differences or dependencies, including any necessary configurations or installations.

8. User Feedback and Error Handling:

When encountering platform-specific issues, provide meaningful feedback and error messages to users. Explain any platform dependencies or specific instructions for troubleshooting platform-related problems. This helps users understand and resolve issues that arise from platform-specific differences.

While striving for portability is important, acknowledging and addressing platform-specific differences allows your script to function optimally across a wider range of systems. By incorporating conditional statements, handling command availability, and accounting for filesystem and environment variations, you can create scripts that gracefully adapt to different platforms while still maintaining overall usability and reliability.

Congratulations on completing **"Shell Scripting 101: A Beginner's Guide to Bash"**! You have journeyed from a novice in shell scripting to a proficient scripter, equipped with the knowledge and skills to automate tasks and unleash the power of the Bash shell.

In this comprehensive guide, we started by laying the groundwork, introducing you to the fundamentals of shell scripting and providing a solid understanding of the Bash shell. You learned how to set up your environment, navigate the command-line interface, and execute basic commands.

From there, we delved into the heart of scripting, covering essential topics such as variables, conditional statements, loops, and input/output operations. You honed your skills in manipulating strings, processing text, and working with files and directories.

Building upon this foundation, we explored advanced concepts, including functions, command-line arguments, regular expressions, and error handling. You gained insights into process management, job control, and automation, enabling you to tackle complex tasks with efficiency.

We also guided you through best practices for writing clean and maintainable code, introduced you to various scripting tools and utilities, and emphasized the importance of debugging and error handling techniques.

Throughout the book, you engaged in hands-on exercises, allowing you to apply your newfound knowledge and reinforce your understanding of each topic. By actively participating in the learning process, you not only absorbed the theory but also developed practical skills that will serve you well in your scripting endeavors.

As you reached the final chapters, you explored the importance of script portability, ensuring that your scripts can run seamlessly across different platforms and environments. This knowledge empowers you to write versatile scripts that can adapt to diverse computing environments.

By completing this guide, you have acquired a valuable skill set that extends beyond the realm of shell scripting. You have developed problem-solving abilities, honed your logical thinking, and cultivated a mindset of automation and efficiency.

With your newfound expertise, you can now automate repetitive tasks, enhance your productivity, and streamline your workflow. Additionally, you possess the foundation to embark on more advanced scripting projects, contribute to open-source communities, and pursue further learning in the vast field of automation.

Remember that mastery comes with practice. Continually challenge yourself to build upon the knowledge gained in this guide. Stay curious, explore additional resources, and tackle real-world problems using the principles and techniques you have learned.

The world of shell scripting is dynamic and ever-evolving, with new possibilities and advancements on the horizon. Embrace this journey as a lifelong learner, continually expanding your scripting skills and exploring the depths of automation.

Thank you for joining us on this exciting adventure through "Shell Scripting 101: A Beginner's Guide to Bash." May your scripts be robust, your tasks automated, and your efficiency unrivaled. Embrace the power of the Bash shell and let your imagination soar in the world of automation!

www.ingramcontent.com/pod-product-compliance
Lightning Source LLC
Chambersburg PA
CBHW071446220526
45472CB00003B/688